# Raw Food Made Easy

## FOR 1 OR 2 PEOPLE

*Jennifer Cornbleet*

Book Publishing Company
Summertown, Tennessee

Cover design:      Warren Jefferson
Cover photos:      Jennifer Girard, Warren Jefferson
Interior photos:   Warren Jefferson
Interior design:   Gwynelle Dismukes

Published in the United States by
Book Publishing Company
P.O. Box 99
Summertown, TN 38483
1-888-260-8458      www.bookpubco.com

Printed in Canada at Transcontinental Printing

ISBN  978-1-57067-175-3

15  14  13  12  11                    14  13  12

On the front cover:
Tropical Fruit Tart, page 156

On the back cover:
California Rolls, page 112

Cornbleet, Jennifer, 1972-
  Raw food made easy for 1 or 2 people / Jennifer Cornbleet.
      p. cm.
  Includes index.
  ISBN 1-57067-175-3
1.  Cookery (Natural foods) 2.  Raw foods. 3.  Cookery for one.
      4.  Cookery for two.  I. Title.
  TX741.C674 2005
  641.5'63--dc22
                          2005019528

Book Publishing Company is a member of Green Press Initiative. We chose to print this title on paper with 100% postconsumer recycled content and processed chlorine free, which saved the following natural resources:

136 trees                    3,787 pounds of solid waste
62,375 gallons of water      12,951 pounds of greenhouse gases
43 million BTU of total energy

For more information visit: www.greenpressinitiative.org.  Savings calculations from the Environmental Defense Paper Calculator on the web at www.edf.org/papercalculator.

To my Spiritual Master and Teacher,

Adi Da Samraj

# Contents

# Acknowledgments

So many friends and students over the years have requested a book of simple, healthy, and delicious raw recipes. They wanted economical, practical, and quick-to-prepare food for one or two people. The dishes had to be familiar tasting and flexible, so that a variety of people, from raw food enthusiasts to traditional diners, could enjoy them. I wrote *Raw Food Made Easy* in response to these desires. My gratitude to all of you.

My heartfelt thanks and appreciation to Keyvan Golestaneh, the holistic health practitioner who introduced me to the raw food diet. Keyvan is a gifted therapist and healer. Working with him showed me the connection between my lifestyle and my physical and emotional health, and helped me heal and become whole. I am truly blessed by his guidance, knowledge, wisdom, compassion, and healing on all levels.

Thanks to Nomi Shannon for teaching the first raw food class I ever attended years ago. After this class, I knew I would teach raw food someday. And thanks to my friend Nicole Freed for encouraging me to follow my passion and for her brainstorming sessions over the years.

My thanks to the staff of Living Light Culinary Arts Institute, including Cherie Soria, Dan Ladermann, David Ross, Patricia Hoskins, Alicia Ojeda, Cassandra Durham, and Julie Engfer. My years as a Living Light student and instructor have been filled with learning, growth, and good times.

Thanks also to Matt Samuelson and Elaina Love, two of the best raw food chefs and instructors around. I've loved trading recipe ideas and working with you over the years, and I look forward to much more.

I am also grateful to Cindy Schwimmer and her family for helping me test many of the recipes for this book and ensuring that they are "kid friendly." Thanks especially to Cindy for her help with my Chicago classes.

Thanks to the staff of the Book Publishing Company for all their flexibility and for making the editing, photography, and publishing process easy and fun. Thanks also to Jennifer Girard for the cover photo of me.

Thanks to the marketing directors of Whole Foods Markets in Chicago, including Joyce Chacko, Kathy Kunzer, Victoria Reed, Sara Parenti, Megan Bowman, Troy Authement, and Elizabeth Boomer, and to Miranda McQuillan of Wild Oats Market, Marc Lapides of Northshore Cookery, Conery Hoffman of Sur La Table, and Karyn Calabrese of Karyn's Fresh Corner, for being so committed to promoting raw food classes in Chicago. Their support has made it possible for me to share raw food with many people.

My most sincere thanks to my parents, Harry and Joanne Cornbleet, and especially to my mother for countless hours of work on my Web site.

Thank you, my dearest Bill, for your rigorous editing, for tasting all my recipes, for your faith in me, for your love, and for making each day together a joy.

Finally, I want to thank my assistants and students in Chicago, especially Connie Lambert, Carol Rodgers, Ellie Welton, Christina Taylor, Belinda Cusic, and Vanessa Sherwood, for inspiring me to teach about raw food and to write this book, and for making it possible to teach so many classes.

# Introduction

A piece of juicy fruit, a crisp green salad, a handful of nuts . . . everyone knows how pleasurable and easy raw food can be. My goal is to help you take the fresh, unprocessed food you already enjoy and expand your options into dozens of easy, inexpensive, delicious meals.

Why eat more raw food? One reason is simplicity. When you prepare food without cooking, you spend less time in the kitchen—in fact you don't even need to be in your kitchen! Whether you are a single person or a couple wanting quick, tasty meals at home, a professional needing a healthy bite right at the office, a student in a dorm without a stove, or a traveler in a hotel, raw is the ultimate fast food.

Another reason to eat more greens, vegetables, and fruits is that they are the easiest way to maintain optimal health and weight. The recipes in this book eliminate the culprits that have been linked to degenerative diseases and weight gain, including "bad carbs" (such as white sugar and white flour) and "bad fats" (such as saturated fats and trans-fatty acids). Additionally, raw greens, vegetables, fruits, nuts, and seeds have vitamins, minerals, phytonutrients, enzymes, and fiber—all essential for good health. Better nutrition will not only help prevent disease and overweight, but will also slow the aging process and increase energy.

Any diet you follow can be improved by eating more green leafy vegetables, less sugar, and less refined food. If you are a vegetarian or vegan, adding raw food recipes will give you more nutrition and variety than cooked vegetables and starches alone. My flexible approach to raw food makes it easier to include them. Only a small percentage of people follow a strict, totally raw diet all of the time, but everyone can improve the meals they already enjoy by adding more raw food.

The simplest raw food needs no preparation whatsoever—you just eat an apple. At the other extreme are elaborate raw dishes that require expensive equipment and unusual ingredients, as well as a lot of advance work (such as sprouting, fermenting, or dehydrating). My book aims at a happy medium between these extremes. The recipes call for only a few pieces of equipment, some of which you may already own, and all of which you can purchase conveniently and inexpensively. The ingredients featured are available at most grocery stores. Preparation techniques are simple, so that a kitchen novice can do fine.

There are hundreds of classic, delicious recipes that could be in this or any other cookbook, but only some recipes are both tasty and easy to prepare. For example, a fruit crisp can be made in 10 minutes, but a layer cake cannot. Guacamole is easier to prepare than avocado salsa. I've chosen recipes that can be made in minutes, that work every time, and that can be eaten every day.

The book is organized into sections on breakfast, lunch and dinner, and dessert, in order to take the guesswork out of what to eat when. Simply turn to the relevant section for guidelines on how to combine the recipes. Eating entirely raw meals will leave you feeling satisfied, yet light. But if you want to add cooked foods to a meal, it is easy to do, and each chapter provides suggestions.

When considering a particular recipe, first note if advance preparation is required, such as soaking almonds or other nuts for several hours. Most of the recipes can be made immediately if you keep a few basics on hand (see Advance Preparation, page 27). Once any advance preparation is complete, get out all the equipment and tools that you'll need and prepare the ingredients as indicated. With everything ready, you will be able to put your meal together in minutes. If any ingredient, piece of equipment, or technique is unfamiliar to you, check the Glossary, page 172, or Tools and Techniques, page 21.

Two last points. 1. The recipes in this book aim to please the average palate, and therefore call for moderate amounts of pungent seasonings, such as garlic, onion, cayenne, and salt. If you like your food highly seasoned, add more of these ingredients; if you don't, begin with small amounts, taste, and adjust up. 2. Recipes for one person are easily doubled to make food for two, or to allow for leftovers. Recipes for two should not be halved, however, because the quantities in these recipes help the blender or food processor work more efficiently. Just save any leftovers for the next day.

# Kitchen Setup

Stocking your kitchen with the appropriate equipment and ingredients will make food preparation easy. The following is a comprehensive list of what you will need. Having these items on hand will allow you to make any recipe in this book. But don't feel that you need to buy everything at once. For many of the recipes, you can get started right away with just a knife, a cutting board, and a few staples.

## Kitchen Equipment

Storing equipment in the part of the kitchen where you will use it reduces movement and increases efficiency. Keep the juicer on the counter by the sink, and the blender and food processor on the counter where you chop. All other tools should be within easy reach of this counter.

### Appliances

blender

coffee grinder (for grinding
  flaxseeds; optional)

food processor

ice cream maker (optional)

juicer

## Bowls, Pans, and Utensils

baking dish, glass (8-inch square)

bamboo sushi mat

cheesecloth or mesh screening (for growing sprouts; optional)

citrus juicer or reamer

colander

garlic press

grater, box

grater, file (Microplane brand; optional)

mandoline (optional)

mason jars, wide-mouth (quart-size)

measuring cups, dry (various sizes)

measuring cups, liquid (1-cup and 2-cup sizes)

measuring spoons

mixing bowls, small and medium

peeler

pie plate, glass (9-inch)

ramekins, two (6-ounce; optional)

salad spinner

saucepan, small (for warming soups; optional)

spatula, rubber

spatula, pie server

sprout bag (for straining almond milk; optional)

strainer, fine-mesh

tart pan with removable bottom (9-inch)

tart pans, two, with removable bottoms (5-inch; optional)

tea kettle (optional)

tongs

vegetable spiral slicer (optional)

whisk

## Knives and Cutting Boards

cutting board, wood or bamboo

honing steel

knife block or holder

knife, chef's (8-inch)

knife, paring

knife, serrated (5-inch)

knife sharpener (optional)

scissors, kitchen

# Kitchen Staples

Stock your kitchen with the items listed that follow, and replenish them as needed. Store nut and seed oils in the refrigerator and extra-virgin olive oil at room temperature. Keep spices and dried fruits in a cool, dark cabinet, away from direct heat and light. Store dates at room temperature for up to two months, in the refrigerator for up to six months, or in the freezer for up to one year. Make sure that you always purchase raw, not roasted, nuts and seeds. Store nuts and seeds in sealed containers in the refrigerator for up to three months, or in the freezer for up to one year.

## Dried Fruits

apples, dried
dates, medjool
figs, Black Mission
mangoes, dried

prunes
raisins, golden
raisins, Thompson

## Frozen Fruits

blackberries
blueberries
cherries

peaches
raspberries

## Dried Herbs and Spices

basil
black pepper
cayenne
cinnamon, ground
cumin, ground

dill weed
garlic powder
onion powder
oregano, dried
paprika

## Oils and Vinegars

apple cider vinegar
balsamic vinegar (optional)

olive oil, extra-virgin

## Raw Nuts and Seeds

almonds
cashews
coconut, shredded dried
macadamia nuts (optional)

pecans
pine nuts
sunflower seeds
walnuts

## Sweeteners and Seasonings

pure maple syrup or agave nectar
miso, mellow white

salt, unrefined
tamari or Bragg Liquid Aminos

## Miscellaneous

almond butter, raw
almond extract
capers
carob or cocoa powder
mustard, Dijon
nori sheets
oat groats, whole

oats, rolled
olives, kalamata, pitted
tahini, raw
tomatoes, sun-dried (dry
   or oil-packed)
vanilla extract

# Weekly Groceries

The following fresh ingredients will enable you to make most of the recipes in this book. The quantities listed are for one person; double them to shop for two.

## Produce

apple, 1
avocados, 2
basil, 1 bunch (about 2 ounces)
bell pepper, red, 1
carrots, 2
celery, 1 bunch
cilantro, 1 bunch (about 2 ounces)
cucumbers, 2
fruit, in season, 3 or 4 pieces
garlic, 1 head

kale, 1 bunch (about 1 pound)
lemons, 2
lettuce, red leaf, 1 head
lettuce, romaine, 1 head
onion, 1
parsley, 1 bunch (about 2 ounces)
spinach, 1 bunch (10 to 16 ounces), or 1 (10-ounce) package baby spinach
tomatoes, 2
zucchini, 2

# Raw Basics

## Why and How to Soak Raw Nuts and Seeds

Some recipes call for unsoaked nuts and seeds because a drier texture is preferred. Soaking raw nuts and seeds in water for several hours makes them easier to process in your blender or food processor, which is important when creating nondairy milks, sauces, salad dressings, and pâtés. Raw nuts and seeds should be soaked long enough to soften them, but not so long that they become soggy and lose their flavor. To soak nuts or seeds, place them in a mason jar. Fill with cool water, screw on the lid, and soak for the specified time at room temperature. If you want to soak sunflower seeds and walnuts longer than six hours, this isn't a problem. They will just be a little less crunchy. When you drain the nuts and seeds, always let them air-dry in the colander or strainer for a few minutes before storing them. This will help retain their crunchy texture and preserve them longer in the refrigerator. Soaked almonds and walnuts keep for five days; soaked sunflower seeds keep for up to three days (after that they may turn a darker brown and taste a little bitter).

### Guide to Soaking Nuts and Seeds

*If a recipe calls for soaked nuts or seeds, measure them after soaking.*

| Nut or Seed | Amount Dry | Soaking Time | Yield Soaked |
| --- | --- | --- | --- |
| Almonds | 1 cup | 8–12 hours | 1½ cups |
| Walnuts | 1 cup | 4–6 hours | 1¼ cups |
| Pecans | 1 cup | 4–6 hours | 1¼ cups |
| Sunflower Seeds | 1 cup | 6–8 hours | 1⅓ cups |
| Sesame Seeds | 1 cup | 4–6 hours | 1¼ cups |
| Cashews | 1 cup | 2 hours | 1 cup |

# Why and How to Soak Dried Fruits

Each recipe that includes dried fruit specifies whether the fruit should be soaked or unsoaked. Dried fruits—such as dates, apricots, figs, and raisins—should be soaked for 10 to 30 minutes when you want to blend them to a smooth consistency for nut and seed milks, puddings, creamy pie fillings, and sauces. If raisins, dried cherries, or dried cranberries are to be used in a salad, they will also benefit from soaking a few minutes, to plump them up. To soak dried fruit, place it in a bowl with enough water to cover for 10 to 30 minutes. Drain well, and use immediately.

Dried fruit in cakes, cookies, and pie crusts should not be soaked, since it will become soggy. Sun-dried tomatoes, if purchased dry, should always be soaked for a minimum of a half hour or up to two hours. Oil-packed sun-dried tomatoes need no soaking.

# How to Store and Ripen Produce

Most fruits, vegetables, and greens can be stored in the refrigerator. Putting them in Evert Fresh Green Bags, specially designed, breathable produce bags (see Kitchen Equipment, page 185), will keep them fresh longer. Bananas and tomatoes, however, should never be refrigerated, since they will turn mushy and lose flavor. Onions and garlic should also be kept at room temperature. Some fruits will continue to ripen after they have been purchased, such as avocados, bananas, pears, plums, peaches, and melons. If they are not ripe initially, store them at room temperature until they are ready. Ripe avocados, plums, and peaches give slightly when you touch them. An unripe melon is rock-hard at the round indentation at the stem end; once ripe, this area is a little softer. Ripe bananas are yellow with brown freckles. Once avocados, pears, plums, peaches, and melons are nearly ripe, move them to the refrigerator if you are not going to eat them right away. They will usually keep for several more days.

If you need to store produce that has already been cut or torn, place it in a resealable plastic bag or Evert Fresh Green Bag, press out as much air as possible, and store it in the refrigerator. Torn greens and the halves of avocado, apple, and tomato will keep for up to two days. (Leave the pit in the avocado half that you are storing and it will retain more of its green color.) Cucumber and red bell pepper halves will keep for up to five days, and onion halves for up to one week.

## How to Clean Produce

Most fruits and vegetables can simply be cleaned with purified water. (See Resources, page 181, for information on purchasing a water filter or distiller.) Produce with a thick skin that will not be peeled requires a vegetable brush for deeper cleaning. Mushrooms should not be washed or they will become soggy. Wipe them off with a lightly dampened paper towel.

Greens require special care, since they usually need to be dried after they are washed. If a recipe calls for whole leaves, clean them with a damp paper towel. This will eliminate the need for drying. To remove the stems from kale or collard greens, hold each leaf upside down by the end of the stem. Grip the sides of the protruding stem with the thumb and forefinger of your free hand. Pull your thumb and forefinger down the length of the stem, stripping off the leaves. For spinach and basil, simply pluck off the leaves with your fingers.

If a recipe calls for torn lettuce, tear the leaves before washing them; then dry them in a salad spinner. You can also wash and dry whole basil and spinach leaves in the spinner. For fresh parsley, cilantro, and dill weed, hold the bunch by the stems and swish it around in a bowl of water. Shake well to dry; then press the bunch of herbs between layers of paper towels to remove any remaining moisture.

# Warming Up Raw Food

Most raw food tastes best at room temperature. Unless a dish is to be served chilled, remove it from the refrigerator 10 to 30 minutes before eating. To warm soup, pour it in a small saucepan and heat it gently for two to three minutes, stirring constantly. To warm a dessert, preheat the oven to the lowest possible temperature (no higher than 200 degrees F). Turn off the oven, insert the dessert, and warm for 15 minutes. Alternatively, heat the dessert for 30 minutes in a food dehydrator set at 105 degrees F.

# Easy Snacks

Some people feel satisfied with three meals a day, while others need a mid-morning and mid-afternoon snack. Snacks should be quick to prepare and easy to transport.

Fresh fruit is a delicious and simple snack. If you have leftover juice from breakfast, you can drink it as a mid-afternoon pick-me-up. For more protein, try soaked almonds (page 17). Combine them with dried figs or dates for a sweet treat, or with cucumber slices if you are avoiding sweets. Macadamia nuts with raisins make a calorie-packed snack that is great for hiking. Almond butter (page 29) is a satisfying spread that can be combined with fruits or vegetables. Try a banana or a stalk of celery spread with almond butter and topped with a few raisins. Or use almond butter as a dip for celery, carrot, and cucumber sticks.

If you prefer five small meals during the day instead of three larger ones, many of the recipes in this book are ideal. At mid-morning, try a raw soup or one of the dips with vegetable sticks. When a sweet craving strikes mid-afternoon, have a guilt-free raw dessert.

# Tools and Techniques

Your most important tools are good quality knives and a sturdy cutting board. A few other pieces of manual equipment and some electric appliances make raw food prep more varied, efficient, and fun.

## Cutting Boards and Knives

Wood or bamboo cutting boards are best. Plastic can chip and leach into the food. Wood also has a bit of give, which makes for easier chopping; plastic is so hard that it can dull your knives. I recommend a large, sturdy board that won't slip. You can buy a second lightweight board for small tasks, if desired. Use one side of your cutting board for fruit and the other for vegetables, to avoid mixing flavors. Clean your boards with a damp sponge and mild dish soap.

An 8-inch chef's knife is essential for slicing, chopping, and mincing harder fruits and vegetables. A good one will last for years. (See Kitchen Equipment, page 185, for recommended brands.) You can purchase a European-style chef's knife or an Asian-style santoku knife, depending on your personal preference. Before deciding, hold each knife to see how it feels.

Learning to slice correctly will save you time and energy. Grip the handle close to where it joins the blade; put your thumb against the side or on top of the blade. Place the knife tip on the cutting board beyond the far side of the fruit or vegetable. Begin cutting with the middle portion of the blade. Push gently down and forward. Pull back and repeat. Use your free hand to hold the fruit or vegetable, with your fingertips safely tucked under.

When mincing onions, garlic, or herbs, use the "fan technique." Gather the chopped ingredients in a pile on the cutting board. Place the tip of the knife on the far side of the pile. Rest your free hand on top of the blade.

Keeping the knife tip on the board, move the blade up and down quickly as you pivot the base of the knife in a fan motion. Stop periodically to regather the pile of ingredients, and continue mincing until the desired texture is achieved. Never scrape the sharp edge of your knife against the cutting board to push the ingredients together; this will dull the blade. Use the back of the knife for any scraping. You can also mince ingredients in a food processor fitted with the S blade. Chop onions or herbs coarsely (peel garlic cloves, but leave the cloves whole) and place them in the processor. Pulse until the desired texture is achieved.

For softer fruits and vegetables—such as tomatoes, mushrooms, olives, citrus fruits, kiwifruit, plums, and peaches—and for slicing California Rolls (page 112), a 5-inch serrated knife or a paring knife is easiest to use. Unlike the chef's knife, these work best if you pull the blade toward you as you slice. A 5-inch serrated knife is also useful for peeling citrus fruits, when you don't want any of the white pith to appear. Cut off each end of the citrus fruit and place the top or bottom of the fruit on a cutting board so it lies flat. Following the curve of the fruit, cut away the peel on all sides. You can then use the knife to remove segments of the fruit by cutting them out from between the white membranes.

Knives require care. Always store them in a block or holder to protect them. To keep your chef's and paring knives sharp, use a honing steel regularly (never use a steel on serrated knives). If the blades get dull, I recommend the Chef's Choice brand multi-edge manual sharpener; it is much easier to use than a traditional whetstone, and it works on both regular and serrated blades. In addition, I recommend having your knives professionally sharpened at least once a year at a cookware, grocery, or natural food store.

A few fruits—avocados, mangoes, tomatoes, and cucumbers—require special consideration. To peel an avocado, place it lengthwise on a cutting board. Cut in with your chef's knife until you hit the pit, then turn the avocado over while rotating your knife all the way around the pit. Give the avocado a twist to separate the halves. Push the lower part of the blade into the pit and twist the knife to pull it out. Scoop the flesh out of the peel with a spoon, then slice or mash.

To peel and chop a mango, slice it lengthwise into quarters, cutting all around the pit. Scoop the flesh away from the peel with a spoon, discard the peel, and slice or chop the flesh. Alternatively, peel the mango with a paring knife, and then slice and chop the flesh.

Tomatoes and cucumbers are seeded in many recipes, as this improves the texture of the finished dish. To seed a tomato, first remove the nub at the stem end with a paring knife. Cut the tomato in half lengthwise. Scoop out the seeds with your thumb and fingers or with a spoon. To seed a cucumber, cut it in half lengthwise and scoop out the seeds with a spoon.

Learning basic knife techniques can greatly improve the appearance of your dishes and make kitchen work more efficient and enjoyable. Learning these skills from books alone can be difficult. See the Resources section (page 181) for recommended classes and videos, or enroll in a knife skills class at a cooking store or school. Most importantly, practice. Concentrate on accuracy, and speed will come with time.

## Other Manual Tools

A box grater is useful for producing small amounts of grated carrot or zucchini; use the shredding disk of a food processor for larger amounts. A file grater (Microplane brand) is wonderful for grating fresh ginger and nutmeg, and for removing the zest from lemons, limes, and oranges.

Besides peeling, a vegetable peeler can make carrot "ribbons" to replace grated carrots in California Rolls (page 112), Garden Wraps (page 111), and Spring Rolls (page 117). To make ribbons, use the peeler to produce long strips, rotating the carrot until there is nothing left to peel. You can make ribbons out of cucumbers and zucchini the same way, peeling them on all sides until you reach the core.

A vegetable spiral slicer, sometimes called a "spiralizer" or a "garnishing machine," transforms zucchini, butternut squash, carrots, cucumbers, beets, parsnips, daikon radish, and celery root into delicate angel hair "pasta." (See Kitchen Equipment, page 185, for where to purchase one.) If you don't have a spiralizer, you can make zucchini "fettuccine" by creating zucchini ribbons with a vegetable peeler.

A mandoline is a great tool for cutting vegetables into ultrathin, uniform slices. There's no need to spend $100 or more on a stainless steel French model; the inexpensive plastic Japanese versions work fine. You can also use a ceramic slicer (Kyocera brand) or a "V-slicer" (Borner brand).

A sprout bag, also called a "mesh bag" or a "nut milk bag," is useful for sraining almond milk and other nut and seed milks (see Kitchen Equipment, page 185, for where to purchase one.) If you don't have a sprout bag, you can use a fine-mesh strainer.

A bamboo sushi mat is essential for making tight, professional-quality nori rolls. They are usually available in natural food stores and Asian markets for a dollar or two.

## Electric Appliances

A blender is the right appliance for making smoothies and creamy soups, sauces, and salad dressings. An inexpensive model is all you need for the recipes in this book, though eventually you may want a high-speed Vita-Mix (see Kitchen Equipment, page 185). When blending, begin with the softest ingredients and some of the liquid. Add the other ingredients and blend until the purée is smooth. Stop occasionally to scrape down the sides of the blender jar with a rubber spatula. Pour in more of the liquid and blend again until you achieve the desired consistency.

A food processor chops, minces, grinds, and makes textured purées. With it you can produce delicious pâtés, chunky sauces, cakes, cookies, and pie crusts. An inexpensive model is fine to start with, but I recommend the Cuisinart brand for maximum performance and durability. A three-cup food processor is ideal for making portions for one or two people. This size will work well for all of the recipes in this book except the cakes, pie crusts, and larger quantities of food, which require at least a seven-cup machine. If you do not have a large food processor, you can process the ingredients for cakes and pie crusts in two batches. All food processors work best if they are filled no more than halfway with ingredients.

Food processors come with an S blade for chopping, mincing, grinding, and puréeing. When mincing, use the pulse button so you don't overprocess the ingredients. For all tasks involving the S blade, you may need to stop and scrape the sides of the bowl with a rubber spatula a few times. Most food processors also come with a slicing disk and a coarse shredding disk. The slicer is useful for large quantities of produce, and the shredder grates carrots and zucchini if you don't want to do it by hand. For extra-fine work, you can special order a 2mm slicing disk and a "fine" shredding disk from Cuisinart to fit your particular model.

There are many types and brands of juicers on the market. They start at about $40, and if you are new to juicing, a basic model is fine. If you use the machine each morning, however, you may want to invest in a slow-speed model designed to extract the maximum juice from greens (see Glossary, page 176, for recommended brands, and Kitchen Equipment, page 185, for sources). These slow-speed models also run at low temperatures, which preserves the nutrients and enzymes in the juice. Juices made in one of these machines can be prepared several hours in advance, without significant loss of nutrients or taste.

# How to Follow Recipes and Measure Ingredients

The ingredients in each recipe are always listed in their order of use. Water is often added last to allow you to thin a recipe to the desired consistency. Avocados and fresh herbs are also often saved for last, since their delicate texture and taste can be adversely affected by overblending.

Before you measure, note how each ingredient is prepped. Is it ground, soaked, grated, sliced, chopped, or minced? Are leaves tightly packed? Are dates pitted? Always prep the ingredients as specified before measuring them. For example, if a recipe calls for "$1\frac{1}{2}$ cups dates, soaked," measure the dates out and then soak them. But if the recipe calls for "$1\frac{1}{2}$ cups soaked almonds," measure them after soaking.

Purchase stainless steel dry measuring cups and spoons for maximum durability. Make sure you always fill the cup or spoon level with the edge. Purchase liquid measuring cups as well as dry, because pouring from them is easier.

# Advance Preparation

Preparing some ingredients in advance each week takes about an hour and allows you to make most of the recipes in this book very quickly. Many dishes call for small amounts of crushed garlic, minced onion, and lemon juice. Since these items keep for one week in the refrigerator, you can save time by preparing larger quantities. Minced parsley and soaked nuts and seeds last for just a few days, so you'll need to prepare them more often than once a week. Almond Milk (page 28) is a tasty milk alternative that you can drink straight, pour on cereal, or use as a base for shakes. Prepare it the day after you've soaked your almonds for the week.

If you want to do more advance preparation, many of the dips, pâtés, sauces, salad dressings, and desserts keep for several days. With two salad dressings and two pâtés on hand, you will be set for the week. Juices, soups, and salads are best prepared fresh, but if you are in a rush in the morning, chop the vegetables the night before.

Many recipes in this book can be used in a variety of ways, so preparing a larger batch in advance doesn't mean you have to eat the same thing every day. For example, Not Tuna Pâté (page 68) can be included in a salad, a Stuffed Bell Pepper (page 121), a Not Tuna Sandwich (page 108), or a Not Tuna Roll (page 113). Walnut Pâté (page 71) can be used in a Walnut Pâté Sandwich (page 108), Not Meat Balls (page 115), or Tomato Stacks (page 119). Chocolate Mousse (page 160) can be eaten straight, layered with Vanilla Crème Sauce (page 166) in a parfait, or used to fill Chocolate Tarts (page 157). As you get familiar with the recipes, you'll discover your own favorites to make in advance.

# Almond Milk

*See photo facing page 41*

*Homemade almond milk is more nutritious than boxed nondairy milks, yet it takes only minutes to make.*

## Equipment

measuring cups
measuring spoons
blender
fine-mesh strainer or
   sprout bag
medium bowl
rubber spatula

Yield: 2 $\frac{1}{2}$ cups, 2 servings

2 $\frac{1}{2}$ cups water
1 $\frac{1}{2}$ cups soaked almonds
3 pitted medjool dates, soaked
$\frac{1}{2}$ teaspoon vanilla extract (optional)

Place 1 $\frac{1}{2}$ cups of the water and the almonds, dates, and optional vanilla in a blender. Blend on high speed until very smooth. Add the remaining 1 cup of water and blend until smooth.

Place a fine-mesh strainer over a medium bowl and pour the almond mixture through it. Using a rubber spatula, stir and press the pulp that is caught in the strainer to extract as much milk as possible. Alternatively, use a sprout bag to strain the milk.

Discard the pulp left in the strainer. Transfer the milk to a sealed container and store in the refrigerator. Almond Milk will keep for five days. It will separate, so shake well before using.

## Variations

• **For Honey or Agave Almond Milk:** Omit the dates and add 2 teaspoons raw honey or agave nectar.

• **For Almond Milk with Stevia:** Stevia is a naturally sweet herb that can be used if you are avoiding fruit sugar and other sweeteners. Omit the dates and add 1 packet ($\frac{1}{4}$ teaspoon) stevia powder or 4 drops liquid stevia.

• **For Almond Cream:** Reduce the total amount of water used to 2 cups. Follow the directions for Almond Milk, but add only ½ cup of water at the end of the blending process (rather than 1 cup).

• **For Sesame Milk:** Replace the almonds with 1 ¼ cups soaked unhulled sesame seeds.

• **For Brazil Nut Milk:** Replace the soaked almonds with an equal amount of soaked Brazil nuts.

# Almond Butter

Yield: ³/₄ cup

1 cup raw almonds, unsoaked
Dash salt

Place the almonds and salt in a food processor fitted with the S blade and process for 5 to 10 minutes, or until the almonds are ground into a paste. Stop occasionally to scrape down the sides of the bowl with a rubber spatula. Stored in a sealed container in the refrigerator, Almond Butter will keep for up to three months.

*You can purchase raw almond butter at most natural food stores, but homemade is more economical.*

## Equipment

measuring cups
food processor
rubber spatula

# Ground Almonds

*Ground almonds can be used to replace flour in cookies, cakes, and pie crusts.*

## Equipment

measuring cups
food processor
rubber spatula

Yield: 1¼ cups

1 cup raw almonds, unsoaked

Place the almonds in a food processor fitted with the S blade and process until finely ground. Store in a sealed container. Ground almonds will keep for one month in the refrigerator or three months in the freezer.

# Frozen Bananas

*Freeze your extra bananas so you will always have some on hand for quick shakes.*

## Equipment

plate
resealable plastic bag

Yield: 4 frozen bananas, 4 servings

4 ripe bananas, peeled

Place the bananas on a plate and freeze for 1 hour. (This will prevent the bananas from sticking together.) Transfer to a resealable plastic bag and press out as much air as possible before sealing the bag and returning the bananas to the freezer. Frozen bananas will keep for up to one month.

# Pressed Cabbage

Yield: 2 cups, 2 servings

$^1/_2$ head green or red cabbage
$^1/_2$ teaspoon salt

Cut the cabbage in half lengthwise. Remove the thickest part of the core with a chef's knife. Separate the cabbage leaves into stacks of 3 to 4 leaves.

Flatten one stack and cut the leaves diagonally into thin shreds. Repeat with the remaining stacks. Alternatively, roll the stacks of leaves tightly like a cigar and put them through the slicing disk of a food processor.

Toss the cabbage and salt in a colander and allow to drain for one hour. Rinse. Press the cabbage lightly to remove excess water, then dry between layers of paper towels. Stored in a sealed container in the refrigerator, Pressed Cabbage will keep for three days.

## Variation

• **For Pressed Cucumbers:** Replace the cabbage with 1 $^1/_2$ peeled and seeded cucumbers, cut into $^1/_4$-inch slices. Toss the cucumbers with the salt in the colander. To soften them further, fill a one-quart resealable plastic bag with water and place it on top of the cucumbers as they drain.

*Salting cabbage gives it a soft, pleasing texture in salads.*

## Equipment

cutting board
chef's knife, 8-inch
measuring spoons
colander
paper towels

# Green Leafy Sprouts

*Many of the recipes in this book call for alfalfa or clover sprouts. You can purchase them in most grocery stores, but it is more economical to grow your own. Sprouting takes five days, but only five minutes of your time per day. Draining the sprouts requires cheesecloth or mesh screening. (This screening, the plastic kind used for windows, is more durable than cheesecloth, and can be purchased at your local hardware store. You can cut it into squares with scissors.) Alternatively, an automatic sprouter would allow you to grow sprouts without any daily attention (see Resources, page 181, for information on where you can purchase one).*

## Equipment

mason jar, wide-mouth, quart-size, with band and lid

measuring spoons

square of cheesecloth or mesh screening

dishrack

medium mixing bowl

Yield: 4 cups, 4 servings

2 tablespoons alfalfa seeds, clover seeds, or a mixture

Place the seeds in a quart-size mason jar. Fill with water and screw on the band with its lid. Soak 8 to 12 hours. Remove the band and lid and place a square of cheesecloth or mesh screening on top of the jar. Screw on the band over the cheesecloth or mesh. To rinse and drain the seeds, pour out the soak water, add fresh water through the cheesecloth or mesh, and pour it out.

Invert the jar on a dishrack, so the seeds can continue to drain. Let the sprouts grow this way for 5 days, rinsing and draining them each morning and evening. On the last day, place the jar by a window for 4 to 6 hours; the sunlight will turn the sprouts green.

Remove the sprouts from the jar and place them in a medium mixing bowl filled with water. Swish them around to loosen their hulls. Holding the sprouts down with one hand, tip the bowl into the sink to drain off the hulls and the water.

Place the sprouts in a colander to air-dry for 30 minutes. Stored in a sealed container or jar in the refrigerator, Green Leafy Sprouts will keep for five days.

Advance Preparation

# Crushed Garlic

Yield: about ¼ cup

**1 head garlic (about 15 cloves)**

$S$eparate the garlic cloves using a chef's knife. To begin peeling, turn the knife on its side; rest your free hand on the blade, and press down on a few cloves at a time. This will crush the garlic enough to loosen the peels. Peel each clove using your fingers.

Crush each clove separately in a garlic press, or mince them all at once in a food processor. Stop occasionally to scrape down the sides of the bowl with a rubber spatula. Stored in a sealed container in the refrigerator, crushed garlic will keep for one week.

*To save time, you can use pre-peeled garlic cloves, which are available in the refrigerated produce section of many grocery stores.*

## Equipment

cutting board
chef's knife, 8-inch
garlic press or food processor
rubber spatula

# Lemon Juice

Yield: about ½ cup

**4 lemons**

$C$ut each lemon in half crosswise. Extract the juice with a citrus juicer or reamer. Stored in a sealed container in the refrigerator, lemon juice will keep for five days.

## Equipment

cutting board
paring knife
citrus juicer or reamer

## Variation

• **For Lime Juice:** Replace the 4 lemons with 8 limes.

# Minced Parsley

## Equipment

medium bowl filled with
   water
paper towels
cutting board
chef's knife, 8-inch
food processor
rubber spatula

Yield: about ¾ cup

1 ounce curly or flat-leaf parsley (about ½ bunch),
   washed and dried

Hold the parsley firmly by the stem end and chop the leaves. Discard the stems or save for Green Juice (page 43). Continue to chop the leaves until they are minced. Alternatively, place the leaves in a food processor fitted with the S blade and pulse until they are minced. Stored in a sealed container in the refrigerator, minced parsley will keep for three days.

## Variation

• For Minced Cilantro: Replace the parsley with an equal amount of fresh cilantro.

# Soaked Oat Groats

**Yield: 2 cups, 4 servings**

**1¹/₂ cups whole oat groats**

Place the oat groats in a small bowl and cover with water. Soak for 8 to 12 hours at room temperature. Drain in a colander and rinse well. Return the groats to the bowl and add enough fresh water to cover. Soak for 8 to 12 more hours. Drain and rinse again. Allow the groats to air-dry in the colander for 30 minutes. Stored in a sealed container in the refrigerator, Soaked Oat Groats will keep for three days.

*Whole oat groats contain more fiber and nutrients than rolled oats. They can be served with Almond Milk (page 28) and fruit, or made into Whole Oatmeal (page 54).*

## Equipment

measuring cups
small bowl
colander or strainer

# Minced Onion

**Yield: about ¹/₂ cup**

**¹/₂ red or yellow onion**

Chop the onion into 1-inch pieces. Place in a food processor fitted with the S blade and pulse until minced. Do not overprocess or the onion may get watery. Alternatively, mince the onion by hand. Stored in a sealed container in the refrigerator, minced onion will keep for one week.

## Equipment

cutting board
chef's knife, 8-inch
food processor
rubber spatula

# Breakfast

A light morning meal will leave you feeling energized and ready to begin the day. Juices and fruits are perfect for breakfast, since they are high in nutrients yet low in calories and easy to digest. If you need something heartier in the morning, try one of the cereals with Almond Milk (page 28). Over time you may find that juice and/or fruit is all you need.

# Juice

Drinking juice each day is the easiest way for busy people to get the vegetables they need. Juices make a cleansing, nutritious breakfast or an energizing mid-afternoon snack. Use organically grown produce whenever possible, especially for greens that can't be peeled, such as kale and celery. Energizing-Purifying Juice (page 40) and Green Juice (page 43) should be your staples, since they are the highest in nutrients and lowest in calories and sugars. The other juices in this section will provide variety during the week. If you are sensitive to sugars, limit your consumption of carrot, beet, and fruit juices, and emphasize ones made from green leafy vegetables. Juicing is a great opportunity to use leftover vegetable scraps from other recipes. Save your parsley stems, broccoli stalks, and other odds and ends, and juice them along with a base of celery, cucumbers, or carrots. For easier digestion and better absorption of nutrients, drink juices on an empty stomach.

A high-quality machine extracts more juice from the produce and preserves more nutrients. (For information on juicers, see Tools and Techniques, page 21, and Kitchen Equipment, page 185.) When you juice, cut the vegetables into chunks that will fit comfortably through the chute of your machine. If you are using a slow-speed juicer designed for greens, do not remove the stems from kale, collards, parsley, and cilantro, or cut them into pieces. Simply feed them, stem side down, into the machine. Start and finish the juicing process with celery or carrots, since they are firm and easy to juice. Don't leave garlic and ginger until the end—juicing other vegetables after them helps push any remaining pieces of garlic and ginger through.

# Apple Juice

Yield: 1 cup, 1 serving

4 apples, cut into chunks

Juice and serve immediately.

## Variations

• **For Apple-Ginger Juice:** Add a 1/4-inch piece of fresh ginger.

• **For Pink Apple Juice:** Use 2 apples (instead of 4). Add 1 beet, 1 peeled lime, and a 1/4-inch piece of fresh ginger.

• **For Green Apple Juice:** After the juice is made, place it in a mason jar. Add 1 tablespoon blue-green algae or green powder, screw on the lid, and shake well.

*Use Granny Smith apples for a tart, less sweet apple juice.*

## Equipment

cutting board
chef's knife, 8-inch
juicer

# Carrot Juice

Yield: 1 cup, 1 serving

4 carrots

Juice and serve immediately.

## Variations

• **For Carrot-Ginger Juice:** Add a 1/4-inch piece of fresh ginger.

• **For Carrot-Celery Juice:** Use 2 carrots and 2 celery stalks.

• **For Carrot-Celery-Beet Juice:** Use 2 carrots, 2 celery stalks, and 1/2 beet.

*Carrot juice and carrot juice blends are excellent sources of beta-carotene.*

## Equipment

juicer

# Energizing-Purifying Juice

Keyvan Golestaneh, a holistic
health practitioner who
introduced me to raw food,
gave this juice recipe to me
several years ago. This juice
detoxifies the body while
providing needed nutrients
and energy. It is a health-
promoting daily breakfast and
an energizing mid-afternoon
snack. There are several
ingredients in this juice, but to
save time you can wash and
cut the vegetables the night
before. For a spicier juice, add
the optional ginger and radish.

## Equipment

cutting board
chef's knife, 8-inch
juicer
citrus juicer or reamer

Yield: $1^{1}/_{2}$ cups, 1 serving

2 celery stalks
1 carrot
$^{1}/_{2}$ cup chopped green or red cabbage
$^{1}/_{4}$ cucumber
4 kale or collard leaves
15 parsley sprigs
$^{1}/_{4}$ cup coarsely chopped broccoli stalk
  (one 4-inch piece)
1 small red radish, or 1 (1-inch) piece daikon radish
  (optional)
1 ($^{1}/_{4}$-inch) piece fresh ginger (optional)
$1^{1}/_{2}$ teaspoons fresh lemon juice ($^{1}/_{4}$ lemon; optional)

Juice the celery, carrot, cabbage, cucumber, kale, parsley, broccoli stalk, and the optional radish and ginger. Stir in the lemon
juice, if desired. Alternatively, peel the lemon and put it through
the juicer with the vegetables. Serve immediately.

See variations on page 41

Mediterranean Kale, page 128, Carrots with Morrocan
Spices, page 124, Stuffed Mushrooms, page 118,
with Sunflower Sun-dried Tomato Pâté, page 72

## Variations for Energizing-Purifying Juice

• **For Sweet Energizing-Purifying Juice:** Add ¼ beet and/or ¼ Granny Smith apple. If using beet, 2 to 3 leaves of beet greens may be added. People who aren't used to the taste of vegetable juice often prefer this sweeter variation.

• **For Soothing Aloe Juice:** Stir 1 tablespoon aloe vera juice into the finished juice. Aloe vera juice is a rich source of amino acids and is soothing to the digestive tract.

• **For Complete Meal Energizing-Purifying Juice:** After the juice is made, place it in a mason jar. Add 1 tablespoon blue-green algae or green powder and 1 tablespoon ground flaxseeds or ground hemp seeds. Screw on the lid and shake well. A small, inexpensive coffee grinder will enable you to grind seeds for your juice.

# Grapefruit Juice

Yield: 1 cup, 1 serving

**2 grapefruits**

Cut the grapefruits in half crosswise. Extract the juice with a citrus juicer or reamer. Serve immediately.

> • **For Green Grapefruit Juice:** After the juice is made, place it in a mason jar. Add 1 tablespoon blue-green algae or green powder, screw on the lid, and shake well.

*Granola, page 52, Almond Milk, page 28, and Berry Smoothie page 47*

*The natural way to get your vitamin C.*

## Equipment
cutting board
chef's knife, 8-inch
citrus juicer or reamer

# Fasting Juice

Yield: 6 cups, 1 full day's supply

*This juice contains the same detoxifying ingredients as the Energizing-Purifying Juice but in larger quantities to make a full day's supply. Diluting juice with water makes it appropriate for a fast. Include the beet or apple if you prefer a sweeter juice. If you are fasting, do not add blue-green algae, green powder, or ground seeds to your juice.*

## Equipment

cutting board
chef's knife, 8-inch
juicer
fine-mesh strainer

2 cups chopped green or red cabbage (about $^1/_2$ head)
1 bunch kale or collard greens (about 16 leaves)
8 celery stalks
4 carrots
1 cucumber
1 bunch parsley (about 2 ounces)
1 cup coarsely chopped broccoli stalks
1 beet (plus the beet greens, if available), or 1 Granny Smith apple (optional)
4 small red radishes, or 1 (4-inch) piece daikon radish (optional)
1 (1-inch) piece fresh ginger (optional)
2 tablespoons fresh lemon juice (1 lemon; optional)
6 cups spring or distilled water

Juice the cabbage, kale, celery, carrots, cucumber, parsley, broccoli stalks, and the optional beet, radishes, and ginger. Stir in the lemon juice, if desired. Alternatively, peel the lemon and put it through the juicer with the vegetables. Strain the juice through a fine-mesh strainer. Dilute the juice with an equal quantity of spring or distilled water, and store it in the refrigerator to drink throughout the day.

# Green Juice

Yield: 1 cup, 1 serving

3 celery stalks
3 kale or collard leaves
$\frac{1}{2}$ cucumber, sliced lengthwise
$\frac{1}{3}$ bunch parsley and/or cilantro (about 1 ounce)
1 ($\frac{1}{4}$-inch) piece fresh ginger (optional)
$1\frac{1}{2}$ teaspoons fresh lemon juice ($\frac{1}{4}$ lemon)

Juice the celery, kale, cucumber, parsley, cilantro, and ginger, if desired. Stir in the lemon juice. Alternatively, peel the lemon and put it through the juicer with the vegetables. Serve immediately.

## Variations

• **For Sweet Green Juice:** Add $\frac{1}{2}$ apple, cut into chunks.

• **For Antioxidant Juice:** Add $\frac{1}{2}$ cup broccoli florets and stalks and/or $\frac{1}{2}$ cup chopped green cabbage.

• **For Complete Meal Green Juice:** After the juice is made, place it in a mason jar. Add 1 tablespoon blue-green algae or green powder and 1 tablespoon ground flaxseeds or ground hemp seeds. Screw on the lid and shake well. A small, inexpensive coffee grinder will enable you to grind seeds for your juice.

*This juice is a nutritional powerhouse, providing vitamins, calcium, and trace minerals. It is also low in calories and sugars, making it an ideal weight-loss drink. For a spicier green juice, include the optional ginger.*

## Equipment

cutting board
chef's knife, 8-inch
measuring spoons
juicer
citrus juicer or reamer

# Lemon Water

*Lemon water is a refreshing and cleansing beverage. Hot lemon water makes a warming drink on a cold morning.*

## Equipment

teakettle, if heating
  the water
cutting board
serrated knife, 5-inch
citrus juicer or reamer
measuring cups
measuring spoons
glass or mug

Yield: 1 cup, 1 serving

1 cup water, room temperature or heated
  in a tea kettle
1 1/2 tablespoons fresh lemon juice

Pour the water into a glass or mug. Stir in the lemon juice and serve immediately.

# Orange Juice

*Orange juice in a carton may be convenient, but it has been pasteurized, resulting in a loss of vitamins and enzymes. Fresh-squeezed orange juice takes just minutes, packs in a full day's supply of vitamin C, and tastes great.*

## Equipment

cutting board
chef's knife, 8-inch
citrus juicer or reamer

Yield: 1 cup, 1 serving

4 oranges

Cut the oranges in half crosswise. Extract the juice with a citrus juicer or reamer. Serve immediately.

## Variation

• For Citrus Sunshine Juice: Use 2 oranges, 1 grapefruit, and 1/2 lemon.

• For Green Orange Juice: After the juice is made, place it in a mason jar. Add 1 tablespoon blue-green algae or green powder, screw on the lid, and shake well.

# V-7 Juice

Yield: 1 cup, 1 serving

*Tastes like a V-8, only better.*

2 celery stalks
1 small ripe tomato, cut into quarters
$1/2$ red bell pepper, cut into pieces
$1/8$ cucumber, cut into pieces
10 parsley and/or cilantro sprigs
1 garlic clove
$1 1/2$ teaspoons fresh lemon juice ($1/4$ lemon)
Dash cayenne or hot sauce (optional)

## Equipment
cutting board
chef's knife, 8-inch
measuring cups
measuring spoons
juicer

Juice the celery, tomato, bell pepper, cucumber, parsley, and garlic. Stir in the lemon juice and cayenne, if desired. Alternatively, peel the lemon and put it through the juicer with the vegetables. Serve immediately.

# *Fruit*

**C**hildren are instinctively drawn to the bright colors, curved shapes, and sweet, juicy flavors of fruit. It is excellent for adults, too, since it is easy to digest, high in vitamins, and a natural way to satisfy our love of sweets. Eat fruit first thing in morning or an hour after your juice. If you are sensitive to sugars, limit yourself to small amounts.

# Applesauce

## Equipment

cutting board
peeler
chef's knife
food processor
rubber spatula

Yield: 1 ½ cups, 2 servings

2 apples, peeled and chopped
4 pitted medjool dates, soaked
Dash ground cinnamon

**P**lace half of the apples and all the dates in a food processor fitted with the S blade and process until smooth. Stop occasionally to scrape down the sides of the bowl with a rubber spatula. Add the remaining apples and the cinnamon and process until smooth. Stored in a sealed container in the refrigerator, Applesauce will keep for three days.

# Berry Smoothie

Yield: 1 ½ cups, 1 serving

See photo facing page 41

*When you're short on time, smoothies make a fast and energizing breakfast. If you like a frosty smoothie, use frozen berries.*

¼ cup water
1 ripe banana
1 cup fresh or frozen strawberries, blueberries, or blackberries

Place all the ingredients in a blender and process on medium speed until smooth. Serve immediately.

## Equipment
measuring cups
blender
rubber spatula

## Variations

• **For Mango Smoothie:** Replace the berries with 1 cup chopped ripe mango.

• **For Orange and Berry Smoothie:** Add ½ orange, peeled and sectioned.

• **For Peach Smoothie:** Replace the berries with 1 cup fresh or frozen peaches.

• **For Goji Berry Smoothie:** Soak ¼ cup goji berries in the ¼ cup water for 30 minutes. Add the goji berries and their soak water along with the remaining ingredients.

• **For Yogurt Smoothie:** Replace the water with ¼ cup plain or vanilla yogurt.

• **For Protein and Omega-3 Smoothie:** Increase the water to 1 cup and add 2 tablespoons protein powder and 1 tablespoon flaxseed oil.

• **For Green Smoothie:** Add 1 tablespoon green powder or ½ cup chopped fresh greens, such as spinach, parsley, kale, celery, or Romaine lettuce.

# Cantaloupe Smoothie

Yield: 1 1/2 cups, 1 serving

1/2 small cantaloupe

Cut the cantaloupe in half crosswise. Using a spoon, scoop out the seeds and discard. Scoop out the flesh of the cantaloupe and place it in a blender. Process on medium speed until smooth. Serve immediately.

## Equipment

cutting board
chef's knife, 8-inch
spoon
blender
rubber spatula

# Piña Colada Smoothie

Yield: 1 1/2 cups, 1 serving

1/2 orange, peeled and sectioned
1/2 cup chopped fresh pineapple
1 ripe banana, fresh or frozen

If using a frozen banana, allow to thaw for 5 minutes. Break the banana into two or three pieces. Place all the ingredients in a blender and process on medium speed until smooth. Serve immediately.

## Equipment

measuring cups
blender
rubber spatula

# Berries and Almond Cream

Yield: 1 serving

1 cup mixed berries (such as blackberries, blueberries, raspberries, or sliced strawberries)
1 teaspoon pure maple syrup or agave nectar
1/2 cup Almond Cream (page 29)

Place the berries and sweetener in a small bowl. Toss gently. Transfer to a wine glass or small dish and top with the Almond Cream. Serve immediately.

*Serve in a wine glass for an elegant breakfast.*

## Equipment

measuring cups
measuring spoons
small bowl
rubber spatula
wine glass or small dish

# Dried Fruit Compote

Yield: 1 to 2 servings

1/4 cup water
4 prunes or dried apricots
1/8 teaspoon lemon or orange zest (optional)
Dash ground cinnamon

Combine all the ingredients in a small bowl. Soak 8 to 12 hours at room temperature. Mash lightly with a fork. Stored in a sealed container in the refrigerator, Dried Fruit Compote will keep for three days.

*Serve this naturally sweet compote plain or with your favorite cereal (pages 51–54).*

## Equipment

small bowl
measuring cups
measuring spoons
file grater (Microplane brand; optional)

Fruit

# Summer Fruit Platter

*A rich array of red, pink, and purple colors makes this fruit platter as beautiful as it is delicious.*

## Equipment

measuring cups
serving platter or plate

Yield: 2 servings

2 small wedges watermelon (optional)
I small bunch red grapes
4 fresh purple figs (optional)
2 plums
$1/2$ cup cherries
$1/2$ cup strawberries

Arrange all the fruit attractively on a platter. Serve immediately.

# Tropical Fruit Salad

## Equipment

cutting board
chef's knife, 8-inch
paring knife
measuring cups
small bowl
spoon

Yield: I serving

I ripe mango, or $1/2$ small ripe papaya, cut into cubes
$1/2$ ripe banana, sliced
I kiwifruit, peeled and sliced
$1/2$ cup raspberries or sliced strawberries
$1/4$ cup Sweet Orange Cream Sauce (page 164; optional)

Combine the mango, banana, kiwifruit, and berries in a small bowl and toss gently with a spoon. Serve immediately, plain or with Sweet Orange Cream Sauce.

# Cereal

Cereal is America's most popular breakfast food. Unfortunately, most boxed cereals are made from refined flour and sugar and have little nutritional value. The cereals in this section use nuts, seeds, and whole grains, and they pack in more flavor than their commercial counterparts. All of the cereals here are served with homemade Almond Milk (page 28), but you may substitute rice milk or soymilk, if you prefer. Plain or maple syrup sweetened yogurt is also a delicious topping.

# Almond Sunflower Cereal

Yield: 1 serving

2 tablespoons soaked raw almonds
2 tablespoons soaked raw sunflower seeds
1 tablespoon soaked raw walnuts or pecans
  (optional)
$^1/_2$ cup chopped or sliced fresh fruit (such as
  apple, banana, berries, kiwifruit, mango, peach,
  or pineapple)
$^1/_2$ cup Almond Milk (page 28)

### Equipment
measuring cups
measuring spoons
cutting board
chef's knife, 8-inch
paring knife
small bowl

Combine the almonds, sunflower seeds, optional walnuts, and fruit in a small bowl. Serve immediately with Almond Milk.

# Granola

*See photo facing page 41*

Yield: 1 cup, 2 servings

## Equipment

measuring cups
measuring spoons
food processor
rubber spatula
cutting board
chef's knife, 8-inch
paring knife
small bowl

¼ cup soaked raw almonds
¼ cup soaked raw sunflower seeds
¼ cup soaked raw walnuts
4 pitted medjool dates, chopped, unsoaked
¼ teaspoon ground cinnamon
Dash salt
½ cup chopped or sliced fresh fruit (such as apple, banana, berries, kiwifruit, mango, peach, or pineapple)
½ cup Almond Milk (page 28)

Place the almonds, sunflower seeds, and walnuts in a food processor fitted with the S blade and pulse briefly, just until coarsely chopped. Add the dates, cinnamon, and salt and process briefly to mix. Store in a sealed container in the refrigerator. Granola will keep for up to two days. When ready to serve, transfer to a small bowl and combine with the fruit. Serve immediately with the Almond Milk.

## Variation

• **For Raisin or Fig Granola:** Replace the medjool dates with ¼ cup raisins or chopped dried figs.

# Muesli

Yield: 1 serving

½ cup rolled oats

2 tablespoons raisins, unsoaked

1 tablespoon chopped raw almonds or walnuts, unsoaked

2 teaspoons raw sunflower seeds, unsoaked

2 teaspoons agave nectar, raw honey, or whole cane sugar

½ cup Almond Milk (page 28)

¼ cup fresh blueberries or sliced strawberries

*Make a large batch of this cereal and store it in your pantry. This way you always have it on hand when a craving for sweet cereal strikes.*

## Equipment

measuring cups
measuring spoons
small bowl
spoon

Place the rolled oats, raisins, almonds, sunflower seeds, and sweetener in a small bowl. Toss gently to combine. Serve with the Almond Milk and berries.

Muesli may be stored in a sealed container in the pantry for up to three months. If you will be storing it, use whole cane sugar instead of agave nectar or raw honey, or add the liquid sweetener just before serving.

## Variation

• **For Soft Muesli:** Soak the muesli in ¼ cup water overnight at room temperature. Serve with the Almond Milk and berries.

• **For a large batch:** Increase the amounts to 4 cups rolled oats, 1 cup raisins, ½ cup chopped raw almonds or walnuts, ¼ cup raw sunflower seeds, and ¼ cup whole cane sugar. Yield: 8 servings, ⅔ cup per serving.

# Whole Oatmeal

*Whole Oatmeal may be served at room temperature or warmed.*

## Equipment

cutting board
peeler
chef's knife, 8 inch
measuring cups
measuring spoons
food processor
rubber spatula

Yield: 2 cups, 2 servings

2 cups Soaked Oat Groats (page 35)
$1/2$ apple, peeled and chopped
2 tablespoons pure maple syrup or agave nectar
2 tablespoons water
$1/2$ teaspoon ground cinnamon
$1/2$ teaspoon vanilla extract (optional)
$1/4$ teaspoon salt
$1/2$ cup Almond Milk (page 28)
2 tablespoons raisins (soaked or unsoaked) or
   Dried Fruit Compote (page 49)

Combine the soaked oat groats, apple, maple syrup, water, cinnamon, optional vanilla, and salt in a food processor fitted with the S blade and process until smooth. Stop occasionally to scrape down the sides of the bowl with a rubber spatula. Serve immediately with the Almond Milk and raisins, or store in a sealed container in the refrigerator and add the Almond Milk and raisins just before serving.

Whole Oatmeal will keep for three days. To warm, heat gently on the stove for a few minutes before adding the Almond Milk and raisins.

# Menus for Lunch and Dinner

For elegance, follow the French tradition of three small courses. This arrangement not only looks attractive, it slows down the eating process, improving digestion. Serve a small bowl of soup or a small plate of salad as a starter. Then present the entrée on its own plate, perhaps with a vegetable side dish or a garnish or sauce. If you are having dessert, serve it on a third small plate, or in a small bowl or ramekin. On the following pages are some ways to put it all together.

# Sample Lunch Menus

Garden Vegetable Soup (page 79)
Veggie Sub (page 109) or Hummus Sandwich (page 107)


Garden Salad (page 88)
Walnut Pâté (page 71)
Creamy Tomato Dressing (page 100)


Greek Salad (page 90)
Garden Wraps (page 111)


California Rolls (page 112)
Cucumbers with Fresh Mint (page 123)


Green Salad (page 91)
Stuffed Tomato with Not Tuna Pâté (page 121)


Papaya Lime Soup (page 82)
Mango and Avocado Salad (page 94)


Spinach Apple Soup (page 83)
Caesar Salad (page 86)

# Sample Dinner Menus

Cream of Zucchini Soup (page 78)
Zucchini Pasta al Pesto or with Marinara Sauce (page 120)
Chocolate Mousse (page 160) with Vanilla Crème Sauce (page 166)


Tricolor Salad (page 96)
Lasagne (page 114)
Marinated Vegetables (page 129)
Flourless Chocolate Cake with Fresh Raspberries (page 138)


Jerusalem Salad (page 93)
Mock Rice Pilaf (page 116)
Carrots with Moroccan Spices (page 124)
Almond Cookies (page 140)


Shaved Beet Salad (page 95)
Stuffed Portobello Mushroom with Sun-dried Tomato Pâté (page 118)
Mediterranean Kale (page 128)
Blueberry Tart (page 154) or Chocolate Tart (page 157)

# Sample Dinner Menus

Miso Soup (page 81)
Spring Rolls (page 117)
Mango Sorbet (page 167) or Key Lime Mousse (page 159)


Gazpacho (page 80)
Stuffed Bell Pepper with Guacamole (page 121)
Latin American Cabbage (page 127)
Tropical Fruit Tart (page 156)


Cream of Tomato Soup (page 77)
Not Meat Balls (page 115)
Coleslaw (page 126)
Apple Crisp (page 147)

# Lunch and Dinner

Raw lunches and dinners need not be limited to salads! For lunch, try one of my blended vegetable soups and a sandwich made with romaine leaves instead of bread. Or if a salad is what you want, make it more substantial and interesting by topping it with a scoop of Guacamole (page 63), Zucchini Hummus (page 73), or Not Tuna Pâté (page 68). Try beginning dinner with a soup, followed by an entrée with a vegetable side dish, and finishing with a dessert.

If you eat cooked foods, there are many ways to combine them with raw dishes. You can choose a cooked soup, or make side dishes from steamed vegetables such as green beans, broccoli, cauliflower, asparagus, or collards. (For some people, these vegetables are too fibrous to eat raw in large quantities, but are easy to digest when lightly cooked.) You may decide to replace the raw entrée with a cooked one, or to add cooked foods to your salad or sandwich. Experiment and you will find the combination of foods that's right for you.

# Dips, Pâtés, and Savory Sauces

All of the dips and pâtés in this chapter make delicious appetizers for any party when served along with Crudités (page 87). If you will be serving people who eat cooked foods, you can bring blue corn chips, whole grain crackers, or pita bread triangles in addition to the crudités. No one will miss the unhealthful mayonnaise-laden dips. Raw dips and pâtés are also versatile staples to make each week and keep on hand. With vegetable sticks, they make easy-to-transport snacks or light lunches. Dips and pâtés also make satisfying fillings for sandwiches (pages 106–109) and hearty additions to salads. Use an ice cream scoop to place a rounded mound of pâté or dip on top of your salad for an attractive presentation. The sauces in this chapter—Marinara Sauce (page 65), Mock Peanut Sauce (page 66), Pesto (page 70), and Olive Tapenade (page 67)— are familiar favorites. If you will be serving others who eat cooked foods, these sauces work as flavorful toppings for cooked as well as raw dishes.

# Guacamole

Yield: $1/2$ cup, 1–2 servings

1 ripe avocado, chopped
1$1/2$ teaspoons minced onion
1 teaspoon fresh lime juice
$1/2$ teaspoon crushed garlic (1 clove)
Dash salt
Dash cayenne

Place all the ingredients in a small bowl. Mash with a fork, leaving the mixture slightly chunky. Serve immediately.

*If you have minced onion and crushed garlic on hand, you can make this classic recipe in five minutes. Serve it with a salad, as a dip with Crudités (page 87), or in a Guacamole Sandwich (page 106).*

## Equipment

cutting board
chef's knife, 8-inch
measuring spoons
garlic press
citrus juicer or reamer
small bowl
fork

# Mock Sour Cream and Chive Dip

*This tastes like "Ranch Dip," only better. Serve it with Crudités (page 87).*

## Equipment

measuring cups
measuring spoons
citrus juicer or reamer
cutting board
chef's knife, 8-inch
blender
rubber spatula

Yield: 1 cup, 4 servings

1 cup soaked raw cashews
$1/2$ cup water
2 tablespoons fresh lemon juice
$1/2$ teaspoon garlic powder
$1/2$ teaspoon onion powder
$1/4$ teaspoon salt
2 tablespoons minced fresh chives or green
   onions
1 tablespoon minced fresh basil
1 tablespoon minced fresh dill weed

Place the cashews, water, lemon juice, garlic powder, onion powder, and salt in a blender and process until smooth. Stop occasionally to scrape down the sides of the blender jar with a rubber spatula. Add the chives, basil, and dill weed and pulse briefly to mix. Chill for at least 30 minutes before serving. Stored in a sealed container in the refrigerator, Mock Sour Cream and Chive Dip will keep for five days.

# Marinara Sauce

Yield: 1 cup, 2 servings

See photo facing page 120

This tastes like the best slow-simmered tomato sauce you've ever had. You can serve it with Zucchini Pasta (page 120) as well as with other entrées, such as Not Meat Balls (page 115).

1 ripe tomato, chopped (about ½ cup)

½ cup sun-dried tomatoes, soaked or oil-packed

½ red bell pepper, chopped (about ½ cup)

2 tablespoons extra-virgin olive oil

1 tablespoon minced fresh basil, or 1 teaspoon dried

1 teaspoon dried oregano

½ teaspoon crushed garlic (1 clove)

¼ teaspoon plus ⅛ teaspoon salt

Dash black pepper (optional)

Dash cayenne

## Equipment

cutting board
serrated knife, 5-inch
chef's knife, 8-inch
measuring cups
measuring spoons
garlic press
food processor
rubber spatula

Place all the ingredients in a food processor fitted with the S blade and process until smooth. Stop occasionally to scrape down the sides of the bowl with a rubber spatula. Stored in a sealed container in the refrigerator, Marinara Sauce will keep for three days.

## Variations

• **For Puttanesca Sauce:** Increase the cayenne to ⅛ teaspoon. Stir 2 tablespoons thinly sliced black olives into the finished sauce.

• **For Middle Eastern Marinara Sauce:** Add a dash of black pepper, ground cardamom, ground cinnamon, and ground cumin.

# Mock Peanut Sauce

Peanut butter is made from roasted, not raw, peanuts, which is why I use raw almond butter for this tasty "peanut" sauce. Serve it with Crudités (page 87) or Spring Rolls (page 117).

## Equipment

measuring cups
measuring spoons
grater
citrus juicer or reamer
garlic press
blender
rubber spatula

Yield: 1 cup, 4 servings

$1/2$ cup raw almond butter (homemade, page 29, or store-bought)
$1/4$ cup water
1 tablespoon fresh lemon juice
2 teaspoons pure maple syrup or agave nectar
2 teaspoons tamari
$1/2$ teaspoon crushed garlic (1 clove)
$1/4$ teaspoon grated fresh ginger
Dash cayenne
Dash salt

Place all the ingredients in a blender and process until smooth. Stored in a sealed container in the refrigerator, Mock Peanut Sauce will keep for five days.

# Olive Tapenade

Yield: $1/2$ cup, 4 servings

1 cup pitted black or green olives
2 tablespoons capers
4 teaspoons extra-virgin olive oil
2 teaspoons fresh lemon juice
$1^{1}/_{2}$ teaspoons minced fresh basil,
   or $1/_2$ teaspoon dried
1 teaspoon crushed garlic (2 cloves)
Dash black pepper

Place all the ingredients in a food processor fitted with the S blade and process until smooth. Stop occasionally to scrape down the sides of the bowl with a rubber spatula. Stored in a sealed container in the refrigerator, Olive Tapenade will keep for five days.

## Variation

• **For Sun-dried Tomato Tapenade:** Replace the olives with soaked or oil-packed sun-dried tomatoes, Omit the capers.

*This topping is easy to make, yet it has a complex, "gourmet" flavor. Use Olive Tapenade as a spread on any sandwich, as a salad dressing, as a dip with Crudités (page 87), or as a sauce for any raw or cooked entrée.*

## Equipment

measuring cups
measuring spoons
garlic press
citrus juicer or reamer
cutting board
chef's knife, 8-inch
food processor
rubber spatula

# Not Tuna Pâté

*This pâté is my daily staple— it's delicious, versatile, and filling. Not Tuna Pâté is the perfect way to turn a salad into a main dish. You can also serve it as a dip with Crudités (page 87) or use it as a filling for Not Tuna Rolls (page 113), Tomato Stacks (page 119), Stuffed Bell Peppers (page 121), or a Not Tuna Sandwich (page 108). You may wish to make a larger batch, since it keeps for five days.*

## Equipment

measuring cups
measuring spoons
food processor
rubber spatula
small mixing bowl
citrus juicer or reamer
cutting board
chef's knife, 8-inch

Yield: $1/2$ cup, 2 servings

$1/2$ cup soaked raw sunflower seeds
$1/4$ cup soaked raw almonds
2 tablespoons water
1 tablespoon fresh lemon juice
$1/4$ teaspoon salt
$1 1/2$ tablespoons minced celery
1 tablespoon minced onion
1 tablespoon minced fresh parsley

Place the sunflower seeds, almonds, water, lemon juice and salt in a food processor fitted with the S blade and process into a paste. Stop occasionally to scrape down the sides of the bowl with a rubber spatula. Transfer to a small mixing bowl and stir in the celery, onion, and parsley. Mix well. Stored in a sealed container in the refrigerator, Not Tuna Pâté will keep for five days.

## Variation

• For Not Salmon Pâté: Add $1/4$ cup grated carrot to the food processor along with the almonds, sunflower seeds, water, lemon juice, and salt. Replace the parsley with 1 tablespoon minced fresh dill weed, or 1 teaspoon dried.

# Salsa

Yield: 1/2 cup, 1 to 2 servings

2 Roma tomatoes, seeded and quartered
1 1/2 teaspoons minced fresh cilantro
1 1/2 teaspoons minced red or green onion
1/2 teaspoon fresh lime juice
1/4 teaspoon crushed garlic (1/2 clove)
1/4 teaspoon minced jalapeño chile, or dash
   cayenne
1/8 teaspoon salt

Place the tomatoes in a food processor fitted with the S blade and pulse a few times to chop. Stop occasionally to scrape down the sides of the bowl with a rubber spatula. Do not overprocess. Add the cilantro, onion, lime juice, garlic, chile, and salt and pulse briefly, just to mix. Allow to stand for 10 minutes before serving to let the flavors blend. Serve immediately.

*With the aid of a food processor, homemade salsa is easy to make! Serve it with Crudités (page 87) and Guacamole (page 63).*

## Equipment

cutting board
serrated knife, 5-inch
chef's knife, 8-inch
measuring cups
measuring spoons
garlic press
citrus juicer or reamer
food processor
rubber spatula

# Pesto

This aromatic sauce gives meals an authentic Italian flavor. It is delicious as a dip with Crudités (page 87), as an ingredient in Zucchini Pasta al Pesto (page 120), Pesto Dressing (page 101), or Tomato Stacks (page 119), and as a topping for any raw or cooked entrée. If you eat cooked food, try the sauce over whole grain pasta. My pesto uses slightly less oil than traditional recipes; increase the oil for a richer sauce.

## Equipment

measuring cups
measuring spoons
garlic press
food processor
rubber spatula

Yield: 1 cup, 4 servings

2 cups basil leaves (stems removed), tightly packed
1/4 cup extra-virgin olive oil
1 teaspoon crushed garlic (2 cloves)
1/4 teaspoon plus 1/8 teaspoon salt
1/4 cup raw pine nuts

Place the basil, olive oil, garlic, and salt in a food processor fitted with the S blade and process until the basil is chopped. Add the pine nuts and process until smooth. Stop occasionally to scrape down the sides of the bowl with a rubber spatula. Do not over-process; you should still see flecks of pine nuts throughout. Stored in a sealed container in the refrigerator, Pesto will keep for five days.

# Walnut Pâté

Yield: $3/4$ cup, 2 servings

1 cup soaked raw walnuts
1 tablespoon fresh lemon juice
1 teaspoon extra-virgin olive oil
1 teaspoon tamari
$1/4$ teaspoon garlic powder
Dash salt
1 tablespoon minced fresh parsley
1 tablespoon minced onion

Place the walnuts, lemon juice, olive oil, tamari, garlic powder, and salt in a food processor fitted with the S blade and process into a paste. Stop occasionally to scrape down the sides of the bowl with a rubber spatula. Transfer to a small mixing bowl. Stir in the parsley and onion and mix well. Stored in a sealed container in the refrigerator, Walnut Pâté will keep for five days.

## Variations

- For Curried Walnut Pâté: Add $1/4$ teaspoon curry powder.

- For Pecan Pâté: Replace the walnuts with an equal amount of soaked pecans.

*This rich, meaty pâté is a good choice when you are really hungry. For a satisfying lunch, have a scoop of it on a Garden Salad (page 88) along with Creamy Tomato Dressing (page 100) or Sweet Mustard Dressing (page 103). You can also serve it as a dip with Crudités (page 87), in a Walnut Pâté Sandwich (page 108), in Tomato Stacks (page 119), or make it into Not Meat Balls (page 115).*

## Equipment

measuring cups
measuring spoons
food processor
rubber spatula
small mixing bowl
citrus juicer or reamer
chef's knife, 8-inch
cutting board

# Sunflower Herb Pâté

*See photo facing page 40*

*This light, delicately flavored pâté tastes good in Stuffed Mushrooms (page 118) and Stuffed Bell Peppers (page 121). You can also serve it with a salad or as a dip with Crudités (page 87). Try the sun-dried tomato variation for an Italian flavor.*

## Equipment

measuring cups
measuring spoons
food processor
rubber spatula
small mixing bowl
citrus juicer or reamer
cutting board
chef's knife, 8-inch
garlic press

Yield: $1/2$ cup, 2 servings

1 cup soaked raw sunflower seeds
2 tablespoons water
1 tablespoon fresh lemon juice
$1/2$ teaspoon crushed garlic (1 clove)
$1/4$ teaspoon salt
Dash cayenne or black pepper
1 tablespoon minced red or green onion
2 teaspoons minced fresh dill weed, basil, or
   parsley

Place the sunflower seeds, water, lemon juice, garlic, salt, and cayenne in a food processor fitted with the S blade and process into a paste. Stop occasionally to scrape down the sides of the bowl with a rubber spatula. Transfer to a small mixing bowl. Stir in the red onion and dill weed and mix well. Stored in a sealed container in the refrigerator, Sunflower Herb Pâté will keep for five days.

## Variation

• **For Sunflower Sun-dried Tomato Pâté:** Add $1/3$ cup soaked or oil-packed sun-dried tomatoes to the food processor along with the sunflower seeds, water, lemon juice, garlic, salt, and cayenne..

• **For Pumpkin Seed Herb Pâté:** Replace the sunflower seeds with soaked, raw pumpkin seeds.

# Zucchini Hummus

Yield: 1 cup, 2 servings

1 zucchini, peeled and chopped
   (about 1½ cups)
2 tablespoons raw tahini
2 tablespoons fresh lemon juice
½ teaspoon crushed garlic (1 clove)
¼ teaspoon ground cumin
¼ teaspoon paprika
¼ teaspoon salt

Place all the ingredients in a food processor fitted with the S blade and process until smooth. Stop occasionally to scrape down the sides of the bowl with a rubber spatula. Stored in a sealed container in the refrigerator, Zucchini Hummus will keep for five days.

## Variation

• For Garbanzo Bean Hummus: Replace the zucchini with 1¼ cups cooked garbanzo beans and add ¼ cup water.

*The inspiration for this recipe came from raw food chef Matt Samuelson's instinct to make hummus with zucchini instead of cooked garbanzo beans. Zucchini Hummus is a little thinner than the traditional garbanzo bean version, but it tastes just as delicious. Serve Zucchini Hummus with a salad, as a dip with Crudités (page 87), or in a Hummus Sandwich (page 107).*

## Equipment

cutting board
peeler
chef's knife, 8-inch
food processor
measuring cups
measuring spoons
citrus juicer or reamer
garlic press
rubber spatula

# *Soups*

If you get tired of chewing salad twice a day, raw soups are an excellent alternative. They are especially nutritious, since blending concentrates a large amount of vegetables into a small volume. Blending also helps break down the fiber in vegetables, making them easier to digest, which is particularly important if you are new to raw foods. The best raw soups are delicately flavored—not too salty, spicy, or rich—so that you can easily eat a whole bowlful. Fruit soups make a refreshing summer meal, and vegetable soups, served at room temperature or warm, can be eaten year-round. To warm a soup, heat it gently on the stove for a few minutes, taking care not to overheat it.

A blended vegetable soup should contain the following components: water, vegetables, fat, citrus juice, seasonings, and salt. The vegetables should be soft, such as zucchini, cucumber, tomato, red bell pepper, or greens. I avoid root and cruciferous vegetables in these soup recipes. Root vegetables, such as carrots and beets, become grainy when blended, and cruciferous vegetables, such as cabbage, broccoli, and collards, are too strongly flavored for raw soups. The best fat to use is avocado—it gets creamy when blended and adds richness without heaviness. You can also add some olive oil for additional flavor and smoothness. Good citrus juices are lemon, lime, and orange; seasonings can include garlic, onion, cayenne, and fresh or dried herbs. To salt the soup, use salt or miso, which adds a deep flavor similar to stock.

To make a raw soup, always blend the water and the softest vegetables first. If you like your soup thick, use less water to begin with. Don't add too much lemon, salt, cayenne, or garlic; you can always spice it up later. Add the greens, avocado, and fresh herbs last, to avoid overblending them. Garnish a raw soup with a drizzle of Ranch Dressing (page 104) or a sprinkle of minced fresh herbs. If you like, you may add a dollop of yogurt. For the best flavor, serve immediately. Or, for a chilled soup, refrigerate for 2 hours before serving. If you need to take the soup with you, transfer it to a glass mason jar. It will keep for up to six hours at room temperature.

# Cream of Cucumber Soup

*Lettuce isn't just for salads— blending it with cucumbers makes a light and delicious summer soup.*

## Equipment

measuring cups
measuring spoons
cutting board
peeler
chef's knife, 8-inch
citrus juicer or reamer
garlic press
blender
rubber spatula

Yield: 2 cups, 2 servings

4 romaine lettuce leaves, chopped (about 1 1/2 cups)
1 cucumber, peeled, seeded, and chopped
  (about 1 cup)
1/2 cup water
1 tablespoon fresh lemon juice
1/2 teaspoon crushed garlic (1 clove)
1/4 teaspoon salt
1/2 ripe avocado, chopped
1 tablespoon extra-virgin olive oil
1 tablespoon minced fresh herbs (dill, mint,
  tarragon, or cilantro), or 1 teaspoon dried

Place the lettuce, cucumber, water, lemon juice, garlic, and salt in a blender and process until smooth. Add the avocado and olive oil and blend again until smooth. Add the herbs and blend briefly to mix. Serve immediately. For a chilled soup, refrigerate for 30 minutes before serving.

# Cream of Tomato Soup

Yield: 1 1/2 cups, 1 to 2 servings

3 ripe tomatoes, seeded and chopped
   (about 1 1/2 cups)
1/4 cup water
1/2 teaspoon crushed garlic (1 clove)
1/4 teaspoon onion powder
1/4 teaspoon salt
1/2 ripe avocado, chopped
1 tablespoon extra-virgin olive oil
2 teaspoons minced fresh dill weed or basil,
   or 1/2 teaspoon dried

Place the tomatoes, water, garlic, onion powder, and salt in a blender and process until smooth. Add the avocado and olive oil and blend again until smooth. Add the dill weed and blend briefly, just to mix. Serve immediately. For a chilled soup, refrigerate for 30 minutes before serving.

*This all-American classic tastes great for lunch, along with a sandwich.*

## Equipment

measuring cups
measuring spoons
cutting board
serrated knife, 5-inch
chef's knife, 8-inch
garlic press
blender
rubber spatula

# Cream of Zucchini Soup

*This soup can be served chilled, at room temperature, or warm.*

## Equipment

measuring cups
measuring spoons
cutting board
peeler
chef's knife, 8-inch
citrus juicer or reamer
garlic press
blender
rubber spatula

Yield: 2 cups, 2 servings

1 zucchini, chopped (about 1 cup)
1/2 cup water, plus 1/4 cup water to thin, if
   necessary
1 celery stalk, chopped
1 tablespoon fresh lemon juice
1 teaspoon mellow white miso
1/2 teaspoon crushed garlic (1 clove)
1/4 teaspoon salt
Dash cayenne
1/2 ripe avocado, chopped
1 tablespoon extra-virgin olive oil
2 teaspoons minced fresh dill weed,
   or 1/2 teaspoon dried

Place the zucchini, 1/2 cup water, celery, lemon juice, miso, garlic, salt, and cayenne in a blender and process until smooth. Add the avocado and olive oil and blend again until smooth. Add the remaining 1/4 cup water to thin, if necessary, and blend briefly. Add the dill weed and blend briefly, just to mix. Serve immediately. For a chilled soup, refrigerate for 30 minutes before serving. To serve warm, heat gently on the stove for a few minutes. Do not overheat.

# Garden Vegetable Soup

Yield: 2 cups, 2 servings

1 small zucchini, chopped (about 1 cup)
1/2 cup water, plus 1/4 cup water to thin, if
   necessary
1/2 ripe tomato, seeded and chopped
1 celery stalk, chopped
1 green onion, chopped
1 tablespoon fresh lemon juice
1 1/2 teaspoons mellow white miso
1/2 teaspoon crushed garlic (1 clove)
Dash cayenne
Dash salt
1 cup chopped spinach or chard
6 fresh basil leaves
1/2 ripe avocado, chopped

*This soup tastes like a green version of Gazpacho (page 80). The basil adds garden-fresh aroma and flavor.*

## Equipment

measuring cups
measuring spoons
cutting board
chef's knife, 8-inch
garlic press
citrus juicer or reamer
blender
rubber spatula

Place the zucchini, 1/2 cup water, tomato, celery, green onion, lemon juice, miso, garlic, cayenne, and salt in a blender and process until smooth. Add the spinach and basil and blend again. Add the avocado and blend until smooth. Add the remaining 1/4 cup water to thin, if necessary, and blend briefly. Serve immediately. For a chilled soup, refrigerate for 30 minutes before serving.

# Gazpacho

## Equipment

cutting board
chef's knife, 8-inch
peeler
serrated knife, 5-inch
measuring spoons
garlic press
food processor
rubber spatula

Yield: 1 1/2 cups, 1 to 2 servings

2 1/2 Roma tomatoes, seeded and cut
into 1/2-inch pieces
1/4 red bell pepper, cut into 1/2-inch pieces
1/4 cucumber, peeled, seeded, and cut
into 1/2-inch pieces
1 green onion, cut into 1/2-inch pieces
1 tablespoon chopped fresh parsley
2 teaspoons extra-virgin olive oil
1/2 teaspoon crushed garlic (1 clove)
1/4 teaspoon salt
Dash black pepper
Dash cayenne
1/2 ripe avocado, diced, for garnish (optional)

Place the tomatoes, bell pepper, cucumber, green onion, parsley, olive oil, garlic, salt, pepper, and cayenne in a food processor fitted with the S blade. Process until blended but still chunky. Stop occasionally to scrape down the sides of the bowl with a rubber spatula. Serve immediately. For a chilled soup, refrigerate for 30 minutes before serving. Garnish with the avocado, if desired.

*California Rolls, page 113*

# Miso Soup

Yield: 1 1/4 cups, 1 serving

1 cup plus 2 tablespoons water

1/4 cup baby spinach leaves, tightly packed

1/4 cup thinly sliced carrot (1/4 carrot)

1 dried shiitake mushroom, soaked 30 minutes in
warm water and thinly sliced (optional)

1 tablespoon mellow white miso

1 teaspoon thinly sliced green onion, for garnish
(optional)

1/4 teaspoon toasted sesame oil, for garnish
(optional)

Place 1 cup of the water and the spinach, carrot, and optional mushroom slices in a small saucepan. Cover and bring to a boil. Immediately remove from the heat and allow to stand for 5 minutes. Combine the remaining 2 tablespoons of water with the miso in a small mixing bowl. Whisk with a fork until blended. Add to the water and vegetables and stir until well combined. Serve immediately, garnished with the green onion and toasted sesame oil, if desired.

*This recipe will satisfy your craving for hot soup during the cold season. The soaked dried mushroom adds a deep, smoky flavor.*

## Equipment

measuring cups
measuring spoons
cutting board
chef's knife, 8-inch
peeler
small saucepan
small mixing bowl
fork
wooden spoon

*Shaved Beet Salad, page 95, with
Lemon Herb Dressing, page 102*

# Papaya Lime Soup

## Equipment

cutting board
chef's knife, 8-inch
measuring cups
measuring spoons
citrus juicer or reamer
blender
rubber spatula

Yield: 2 cups, 2 servings

1 small ripe papaya
1/2 ripe mango, chopped (about 1/2 cup)
2 tablespoons fresh orange juice
   (about 1/2 orange)
1 tablespoon fresh lime juice
2 strawberries

Cut the papaya in half lengthwise and remove the seeds with a spoon. Scoop out the flesh and chop coarsely (this will make about 2 cups). Place in a blender with the mango, orange juice, lime juice, and strawberries and process until smooth. Serve immediately. For a chilled soup, refrigerate for 30 minutes before serving.

# Spinach Apple Soup

Yield: 1 1/2 cups, 1 serving

2 cups spinach leaves, tightly packed
1/2 apple, peeled and chopped
1/2 cup water, plus 1/4 cup water to thin, if
   necessary
1 teaspoon fresh lemon juice
Dash salt
1/2 ripe avocado, chopped

## Equipment

measuring cups
measuring spoons
cutting board
peeler
chef's knife, 8-inch
citrus juicer or reamer
blender
rubber spatula

Place the spinach, apple, water, lemon juice, and salt in a blender and process until smooth. Add the avocado and process until smooth. Add the remaining 1/4 cup water to thin, if necessary, and blend briefly. Serve immediately. For a chilled soup, refrigerate for 30 minutes before serving.

## Variation

• **For Chard or Kale Apple Soup:** Replace the spinach with 2 cups chopped chard or kale.

# Salads

Any diet can be improved by adding a leafy green salad each day. A great salad begins with fresh organic red or green leaf lettuce, romaine, and/or mesclun. You can also include spicier greens, such as arugula, watercress, and frisée, and small amounts of other sliced or grated vegetables, such as tomatoes, cucumbers, and carrots. Leaf lettuces and mesclun are best used within a few days; I recommend buying smaller amounts twice a week to ensure freshness. Storing these delicate greens in Evert Fresh Green Bags will keep them fresh for several days (see Kitchen Equipment, page 185). Alternatively, use romaine lettuce in your salads during the latter part of the week, since it keeps longer. For crispy and tasty romaine salads, remove the wilted outer leaves from the head, or buy romaine hearts, which are often available in convenient packages of three.

To prepare a green salad, first tear all the lettuce into bite-size pieces and place it in a salad spinner. Fill the spinner with water and swirl the greens around using your hands. Lift out the spinner's insert and pour the water from the base bowl. Place the insert back into the bowl and spin the greens dry. Transfer the greens to a large salad bowl and add any other salad ingredients. A mandoline is a handy tool for preparing accompaniments, such as thinly sliced cucumbers and onions.

Toss the salad with the dressing of your choice. Serve it directly from the bowl, or for an attractive presentation, arrange individual servings on salad plates. You may wish to reserve some of the sliced or grated accompaniments to garnish each plate. To make a salad into a one-dish meal, top it with a scoop of dip or pâté. Or, if you eat cooked foods, add some leftover steamed vegetables, whole grains, or beans. If you eat dairy products, raw milk cheese or goat cheese complements green salads nicely.

You can make salads as far as 12 hours in advance—just don't toss them with dressing until you are ready to serve them. If you need to carry a main-dish salad with you during the day, place two tablespoons of dressing in the bottom of a glass mason jar. Add raw or steamed vegetables, such as broccoli, asparagus, green beans, or other cooked ingredients, if desired. Place the lettuce on top of these ingredients, which will absorb the flavor of the dressing and prevent the lettuce from wilting. When you are ready to serve the salad, invert the jar onto a plate; the lettuce will be on the bottom, and the marinated ingredients will be on top.

# Caesar Salad

*My version of this salad looks just like the traditional Caesar, but replaces the egg yolk and anchovies with a delicious vegan ranch dressing.*

## Equipment

mandoline (optional)

cutting board

chef's knife, 8-inch

salad spinner

serrated knife, 5-inch

measuring cups

measuring spoons

medium or large mixing bowl

tongs

serving plate

Yield: 1 serving

1/2 head romaine lettuce, or 1 romaine heart

2 tablespoons Ranch Dressing (page 104)

1/2 Roma tomato, seeded and diced

6 very thin slices red onion (optional)

2 tablespoons thinly sliced black olives

Freshly ground black pepper (optional)

Remove any wilted outer leaves from the romaine. Slice the remaining leaves into 1-inch strips. Using a salad spinner, wash and dry the strips. Place the romaine and the Ranch Dressing in a mixing bowl and toss well. Transfer to a serving plate and top with the tomato, optional red onion, olives, and optional pepper. Serve immediately.

Note: To thinly slice the onion, use a mandoline or a sharp knife.

# Crudités

Yield: 1 serving

½ carrot, peeled
½ celery stalk
¼ cucumber, peeled and seeded
½ red bell pepper
4 broccoli florets
4 cherry tomatoes

Slice the carrot, celery, and cucumber on the diagonal into chip shapes. Cut the red bell pepper half into six chunks. Arrange the carrot, celery, cucumber, and red bell pepper in a circle on a serving plate, and place the broccoli florets and cherry tomatoes in the center. Serve immediately or store the vegetables in a sealed container in the refrigerator. Crudités will keep for up to three days.

*Crudités is the French word for cut-up raw veggies. This colorful combination, cut into attractive chip shapes, works for both a daily snack and a fancy party platter (just increase the quantities as needed). Serve with any dip, pâté, or salad dressing.*

## Equipment
cutting board
chef's knife, 8-inch
peeler
serving plate

# Garden Salad

*This nutrition-packed salad is my daily staple. It can be simple or deluxe, depending on how many optional ingredients are added.*

Yield: 1 serving

## Equipment

salad spinner

measuring cups

cutting board

peeler

chef's knife, 8-inch

grater, or food processor fitted with a shredding disk

mandoline (optional)

medium mixing bowl

tongs

## Basic Salad

1 cup torn red leaf lettuce

1 cup torn romaine lettuce

$1/2$ ripe avocado, cubed

$1/4$ cucumber, thinly sliced

$1/4$ carrot, grated or thinly sliced

## Optional Additions

1 cup baby spinach

$1/2$ cup alfalfa or clover sprouts

$1/4$ cup thinly sliced red or green onion

$1/4$ zucchini, grated or thinly sliced

$1/4$ celery stalk, thinly sliced

2 cherry tomatoes, halved

2 tablespoons soaked raw sunflower seeds

2 tablespoons sliced olives

2 tablespoons dulse flakes

Combine all the basic ingredients in a mixing bowl, adding as many optional ingredients as you like. Toss with about 2 tablespoons of the dressing of your choice. Serve immediately.

**Note:** To slice the cucumber, carrot, and zucchini very thinly, use a mandoline or a sharp knife.

# Grapefruit and Avocado Salad

Yield: 1 serving

1 grapefruit
2 cups torn red leaf lettuce
1 cup arugula (optional)
2 tablespoons Lemon Herb Dressing plus extra
   for drizzling (page 102)
1/2 ripe avocado, thinly sliced

Using a 5-inch serrated knife, cut off the top and bottom of the grapefruit. Then use the knife to remove the peel and white pith and separate the grapefruit into segments. Place the red leaf lettuce and arugula in a mixing bowl. Add the dressing and toss gently. Transfer to a serving plate and arrange the grapefruit and avocado on top. Drizzle with additional dressing. Serve immediately.

## Equipment

cutting board
serrated knife, 5-inch
salad spinner
measuring cups
measuring spoons
chef's knife, 8-inch
medium mixing bowl
tongs
serving plate

# Greek Salad

Enjoy this salad as a delicious
first course before Mock Rice
Pilaf (page 116) or Garden
Wraps (page 111).

## Equipment

cutting board

serrated knife, 5-inch

chef's knife, 8-inch

mandoline (optional)

salad spinner

measuring spoons

medium or large mixing
   bowl

tongs

Yield: 1 serving

2 cups torn romaine lettuce

1 Roma tomato, seeded and cut into chunks

1/4 cucumber, seeded and cubed

1/4 cup thinly sliced red onion

1/4 red bell pepper, cut into chunks

2 to 3 tablespoons Lemon Herb Dressing
   (page 102)

2 tablespoons sliced kalamata olives

Place all the ingredients in a mixing bowl and toss well to combine. Serve immediately.

## Variation

• For Greek Salad with Feta: Add 1/4 cup cubed or crumbled feta cheese.

Note: To slice the onion very thinly, use a mandoline or a sharp knife.

# Green Salad

Yield: I serving

2 cups mixed lettuces (red leaf, green leaf, romaine, Bibb)

I tablespoon Classic Vinaigrette (page 99), Lemon Herb Dressing (page 102), or Sweet Mustard Dressing (page 103)

4 thin slices Roma tomato, cucumber, or carrot, for garnish (optional)

Place the lettuce and dressing in a mixing bowl and toss gently. Transfer to a serving plate. Garnish with the tomato, cucumber, or carrot, if desired. Serve immediately.

## Variation

• For Green Salad with Avocado or Cheese: Add $1/2$ avocado, sliced, or 2 tablespoons goat cheese or feta cheese.

*Sometimes simple is best, especially when a salad will be followed by a more elaborate meal.*

## Equipment

salad spinner
measuring cups
measuring spoons
medium mixing bowl
tongs
serving plate

# Harvest Salad

This salad makes a delicious first course for a fall or winter meal.

## Equipment

salad spinner
medium mixing bowl
measuring cups
measuring spoons
tongs
serving plate
cutting board
chef's knife, 8-inch

Yield: 1 serving

2 cups torn red leaf lettuce or mesclun
$1/4$ apple or ripe pear, thinly sliced
2 tablespoons Classic Vinaigrette (page 99)
1 tablespoon chopped pecans, unsoaked
1 tablespoon fresh raspberries, dried cherries, or
    dried cranberries (see note)

Place the lettuce, apple, and vinaigrette in a mixing bowl and toss gently. Transfer to a serving plate and arrange the pecans and raspberries on top. Serve immediately.

## Variation

• For Harvest Salad with Cheese: Add 2 tablespoons blue cheese, such as Roquefort or Gorgonzola.

Note: If using dried cherries or cranberries, soak them in water for 10 minutes to plump them, then drain well.

# Jerusalem Salad

Yield: 1 serving

½ cucumber, seeded and diced
½ tomato, seeded and diced
2 tablespoons Lemon Herb Dressing (page 102)
   or Tahini Lemon Dressing (page 105)
1 tablespoon minced onion
1 tablespoon minced fresh parsley

Place all the ingredients in a mixing bowl and toss to combine. Serve immediately.

*This traditional salad is served in most Middle Eastern restaurants. It makes a good accompaniment to Zucchini Hummus (page 73).*

## Equipment

cutting board
chef's knife, 8-inch
measuring spoons
small mixing bowl
rubber spatula

# Mango and Avocado Salad

*Serve this salad with Papaya Lime Soup (page 82) for a tropical summer lunch.*

## Equipment

cutting board
chef's knife, 8-inch
measuring cups
measuring spoons
citrus juicer or reamer
small mixing bowl
rubber spatula
salad spinner
serving plate

Yield: 1 serving

1 ripe mango, cubed
1/2 ripe avocado, cubed
2 teaspoons minced red onion
1 teaspoon minced fresh cilantro
1 teaspoon fresh lime juice
1/4 teaspoon minced jalapeño chile, or dash cayenne
2 cups mesclun or shredded romaine lettuce
2 tablespoons Lime Herb Dressing (page 102)

Place the mango, avocado, onion, cilantro, lime juice, and chile in a mixing bowl and toss gently. Arrange the mesclun on a serving plate and drizzle with the Lime Herb Dressing. Using a rubber spatula, mound the mango-avocado mixture in the center of the plate. Serve immediately.

# Shaved Beet Salad

Yield: 1 serving

*See photo facing page 81*

½ small beet, peeled (see note below)
3 tablespoons Lemon Herb Dressing (page 102)
2 cups mesclun or arugula
1 tablespoon chopped raw walnuts, unsoaked
(optional)

*Marinating thinly sliced raw beets in Lemon Herb Dressing makes them tender and delicious; it also imparts a beautiful fuchsia color to the dressing.*

Slice the beet paper-thin using a mandoline or a sharp knife. Place in a mixing bowl, add the dressing, and toss until evenly coated. Marinate for 30 minutes at room temperature, or up to 12 hours in the refrigerator. Arrange the mesclun on a serving plate. Remove the beets from the dressing and place on top of the greens along with the walnuts, if desired. Drizzle with the remaining dressing left from marinating the beets. Serve immediately.

## Equipment

cutting board
chef's knife, 8-inch
peeler
mandoline (optional)
measuring cups
measuring spoons
small mixing bowl
rubber spatula
tongs
serving plate

## Variation

• **For Shaved Beet Salad with Cheese:** Add 2 tablespoons blue cheese, such as Roquefort or Gorgonzola.

**Note:** To peel a beet, slice off the top and bottom, then remove the peel with a sharp vegetable peeler, such as Oxo brand.

# Tricolor Salad

*This elegant salad is worth the extra expense of the radicchio and Belgian endive, two gourmet greens that can be found in most supermarkets.*

## Equipment

cutting board

chef's knife, 8-inch

measuring cups

measuring spoons

salad spinner

medium or large mixing
  bowl

tongs

serving plate

serving plate

Yield: 1 serving

1 cup baby spinach or arugula

3/4 cup chopped Belgian endive (about 2 heads)

3/4 cup chopped radicchio (about 1/4 head)

2 tablespoons Classic Vinaigrette (page 99)

1 tablespoon chopped walnuts, unsoaked

Place the spinach, Belgian endive, radicchio, and vinaigrette in a mixing bowl. Lightly massage the greens for a minute with your hands to soften them. Transfer to a serving plate and top with the walnuts. Serve immediately.

## Variation

• For Tricolor Salad with Goat Cheese: Top with a piece of fresh goat cheese.

# Caprese Salad

Yield: 1 serving

2 ripe tomatoes, thinly sliced
$^1/_8$ teaspoon salt
1 tablespoon minced fresh basil or oregano
2 teaspoons extra-virgin olive oil

Arrange the tomatoes on a serving plate. Sprinkle with the salt and minced basil. Drizzle with the olive oil and serve immediately.

## Variation

• **For Caprese Salad with Goat Cheese:** Add 2 ounces fresh goat cheese.

*When they are available, multicolored heirloom tomatoes make this simple salad beautiful.*

## Equipment

cutting board
chef's knife, 8-inch
serrated knife, 5-inch
measuring spoons
serving plate

# Salad Dressings

Lemon Herb Dressing is my favorite in this section, because it highlights the delicate flavors of greens without overpowering them. The other salad dressings in this section provide variety and are especially delicious if you like creamy textures. For a rich dressing, try my Ranch (page 104). You won't miss the mayonnaise and sour cream. And if you're cutting back on fat, Creamy Cucumber (page 100) will give you flavor without too much oil.

For a simple dressing, drizzle a little extra-virgin olive oil on your salad, toss, add a little lemon or lime juice, and toss again. That's it! You can also use nut and seed oils, such as walnut, flaxseed, and pumpkin seed, instead of olive oil.

# Classic Vinaigrette

Yield: 1/4 cup, 2 servings

1 tablespoon apple cider vinegar or balsamic
  vinegar
1/2 teaspoon Dijon mustard (optional)
1/8 teaspoon salt
Dash black pepper (optional)
3 tablespoons extra-virgin olive oil

Place the vinegar, mustard, salt, and pepper in a small mixing bowl and whisk to combine. Add the olive oil and whisk until smooth. Stored in a cruet or glass jar in the refrigerator, Classic Vinaigrette will keep for one week.

## Variation

• For Classic Vinaigrette with Herbs and Shallots: Add 1/2 teaspoon minced fresh parsley and 1/2 teaspoon minced shallots.

*Apple cider vinegar is easier to digest than red wine vinegars, and it has a fine fruity flavor. For a more traditional taste, substitute balsamic vinegar.*

## Equipment

measuring spoons
small mixing bowl
whisk

# Creamy Cucumber Dressing

*This dressing is so creamy, you'll never guess it's low fat.*

## Equipment

cutting board
peeler
chef's knife, 8-inch
measuring cups
measuring spoons
garlic press
citrus juicer or reamer
blender
rubber spatula

Yield: 1 cup, 4 servings

1 small cucumber, peeled, seeded, and chopped (about 1 cup)
$1/4$ cup extra-virgin olive oil
$1 1/2$ tablespoons fresh lemon juice
$1/4$ teaspoon salt
$1/4$ teaspoon crushed garlic ($1/2$ clove)
Dash cayenne (optional)
$1 1/2$ teaspoons minced fresh dill weed or basil, or $1/2$ teaspoon dried
1 teaspoon minced red or yellow onion

Place the cucumber, olive oil, lemon juice, salt, garlic, and cayenne in a blender and process until smooth and creamy. Add the dill weed and onion and blend briefly, just to mix. Stored in a cruet or glass jar in the refrigerator, Creamy Cucumber Dressing will keep for three days.

## Variations

• For Creamy Red Bell Pepper Dressing: Replace the cucumber with 1 small red bell pepper, chopped (about 1 cup).

• For Creamy Tomato Dressing: Replace the cucumber with 2 ripe tomatoes, seeded and chopped (about 1 cup). Reduce the lemon juice to 1 tablespoon.

# Pesto Dressing

Yield: ½ cup, 2 servings

½ cup Pesto (page 70)
2 tablespoons fresh lemon juice

Place the pesto and lemon juice in a small bowl and stir to combine. Stored in a sealed container in the refrigerator, Pesto Dressing will keep for five days.

measuring cups
measuring spoons
small mixing bowl
citrus juicer or reamer
spoon

# Lemon Herb Dressing

*See photo facing page 81*

*This is my favorite salad dressing. It adds zing and fragrance to a salad, without overpowering the delicate flavors of the greens. Moreover, the taste can be varied easily by changing the fresh herbs.*

## Equipment

measuring cups
measuring spoons
citrus juicer or reamer
garlic press
cutting board
chef's knife, 8-inch
small mixing bowl
whisk

Yield: $3/4$ cup, 4 servings

$1/4$ cup fresh lemon juice
1 tablespoon minced fresh herbs (parsley, basil, dill, mint, tarragon, or oregano)
$1/2$ teaspoon crushed garlic (1 clove)
$1/4$ teaspoon plus $1/8$ teaspoon salt
$1/4$ teaspoon Dijon mustard (optional)
Dash black pepper (optional)
$1/2$ cup extra-virgin olive oil

Place the lemon juice, herbs, garlic, salt, mustard, and pepper in small bowl and whisk to combine. Add the olive oil and whisk again until well blended. Stored in a cruet or glass jar in the refrigerator, Lemon Herb Dressing will keep for five days.

## Variations

• For Lime Herb Dressing: Replace the lemon juice with an equal amount of fresh lime juice.

• For Spicy Cilantro Lime Dressing: Replace the lemon juice with an equal amount of fresh lime juice. Use cilantro as the fresh herb. Add $1/8$ teaspoon cayenne and a dash of ground cumin.

# Sweet Mustard Dressing

Yield: ³/₄ cup, 4 servings

½ cup extra-virgin olive oil
¼ cup apple cider vinegar or fresh lemon juice
1 tablespoon Dijon mustard
2 teaspoons agave nectar or raw honey
¼ teaspoon plus ⅛ teaspoon salt
½ teaspoon crushed garlic (1 clove)
Dash black pepper

## Equipment

citrus juicer or reamer
measuring cups
measuring spoons
garlic press
blender
rubber spatula

Place all the ingredients in a blender and process until smooth and creamy. Stored in a cruet or glass jar in the refrigerator, Sweet Mustard Dressing will keep for one week.

# Ranch Dressing

*This dressing tastes so rich
and creamy, you won't
believe it's dairy free.*

## Equipment

measuring cups
measuring spoons
citrus juicer or reamer
cutting board
chef's knife, 8-inch
blender
rubber spatula

Yield: 1 cup, 4 servings

1 cup soaked raw cashews
$3/4$ cup water
2 tablespoons fresh lemon juice
$1/2$ teaspoon garlic powder
$1/2$ teaspoon onion powder
$1/4$ teaspoon plus $1/8$ teaspoon salt
1 tablespoon minced fresh basil, or 1 teaspoon
  dried
1 tablespoon minced fresh dill weed, or
  1 teaspoon dried

Place the cashews, water, lemon juice, garlic powder, onion powder, and salt in a blender and process until smooth and creamy. Add the basil and dill weed and pulse briefly, just to mix. Stored in a sealed container in the refrigerator, Ranch Dressing will keep for five days.

## Variation

• For Thousand Island Dressing: Add $1/2$ chopped red bell pepper (about $1/2$ cup) to the blender along with the other ingredients.

# Tahini Lemon Dressing

Yield: 1 cup, 4 servings

1/2 cup raw tahini
1/3 cup water
1/4 cup fresh lemon juice
1/2 teaspoon crushed garlic (1 clove)
1/4 teaspoon ground cumin
1/4 teaspoon salt
Dash cayenne
1 tablespoon minced fresh parsley

Place the tahini, water, lemon juice, garlic, cumin, salt, and cayenne in a blender and process until smooth. Add the parsley and pulse briefly, just to mix. Stored in a sealed container in the refrigerator, Tahini Lemon Dressing will keep for five days.

*This dressing will add a Middle Eastern flavor to Garden Salad (page 88) or Jerusalem Salad (page 93).*

## Equipment

measuring cups
measuring spoons
citrus juicer or reamer
garlic press
blender
rubber spatula

# 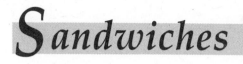Sandwiches

A sandwich is such a convenient lunch because you can eat it with your hands, it's portable, and it fills you up. But with two pieces of bread, a typical sandwich is a high-carb meal that can leave you feeling tired and sluggish. To cut the carbs, replace the bread with romaine lettuce. Just spread one leaf with leftover pâté, dip, or avocado, add some sprouts and tomato slices, and place another romaine leaf on top. If you are taking the sandwich with you, wrap it in plastic wrap and put it in a lunch bag or box. You can eat it with your hands, just like a traditional sandwich.

# Guacamole Sandwich

## Equipment

rubber spatula
cutting board
serrated knife, 5-inch

Yield: 1 serving

2 large romaine lettuce leaves
$\frac{1}{2}$ cup Guacamole (page 63)
$\frac{1}{2}$ Roma tomato, sliced

Spread one of the romaine leaves with the guacamole, and arrange the tomato over it. Put the second romaine leaf on top. Serve immediately.

# Hummus Sandwich

Yield: 1 serving

2 large romaine lettuce leaves
$1/2$ cup Zucchini Hummus (page 73)
$1/4$ red bell pepper, sliced into rings
2 tablespoons sliced black olives

Equipment

rubber spatula
cutting board
serrated knife, 5-inch
chef's knife, 8-inch

Spread one of the romaine leaves with the hummus, and arrange the red bell pepper and black olives over it. Put the second romaine leaf on top. Serve immediately.

## Variation

• **For Hummus Sandwich with Feta:** Sprinkle 2 tablespoons crumbled feta cheese over the olives.

# Not Tuna Sandwich

## Equipment

rubber spatula
cutting board
serrated knife, 5-inch
chef's knife, 8-inch

Yield: I serving

2 large romaine lettuce leaves
1/4 cup Not Tuna Pâté (page 68)
I cup alfalfa or clover sprouts
6 slices cucumber
I Roma tomato, sliced

Spread one of the romaine leaves with the pâté, and arrange the sprouts, cucumber, and tomato over it. Put the second romaine leaf on top. Serve immediately.

# Walnut Pâté Sandwich

## Equipment

rubber spatula
cutting board
serrated knife, 5-inch

Yield: I serving

2 romaine lettuce leaves
1/4 cup Walnut Pâté (page 71)
I cup alfalfa or clover sprouts
I Roma tomato, sliced
I tablespoon Sweet Mustard Dressing (page 103; optional)

Spread one of the romaine leaves with the pâté, and arrange the sprouts and tomato over it. Drizzle with the dressing, if desired. Put the second romaine leaf on top. Serve immediately.

# Veggie Sub Sandwich

Yield: 1 serving

2 large romaine lettuce leaves
1 cup alfalfa or clover sprouts
$^{1}/_{2}$ ripe avocado, sliced
6 thin slices cucumber
$^{1}/_{2}$ Roma tomato, sliced
6 thin slices onion
1 tablespoon Lemon Herb Dressing (page 102)
   or Ranch Dressing (page 104)

## Equipment

cutting board
serrated knife, 5-inch
chef's knife, 8-inch
mandoline (optional)

Arrange the sprouts, avocado, cucumber, tomato, and onion on one leaf of the romaine. Drizzle with the dressing. Put the second romaine leaf on top. Serve immediately.

Note: To thinly slice the cucumber and onion, use a mandoline or a sharp knife.

# *Entrées*

No matter how delicious a raw soup or salad is, you may desire a good main dish as well. You don't have to spend hours making dehydrated mock pizzas or mock burgers to provide a raw entrée. With only a few greens or vegetables and some leftover pâté or dip, you can use the techniques of stacking, stuffing, and rolling to create an elegant entrée in a matter of minutes. Stacking transforms tomatoes and Pesto (page 70) into Tomato Stacks (page 119), and zucchini slices, spinach, and Marinara Sauce (page 65) into Lasagne (page 114). If you have Not Tuna Pâté (page 68) or Guacamole (page 63) on hand, you can make Stuffed Bell Peppers (page 121), Stuffed Tomatoes (page 121), or Stuffed Mushrooms (page 118) in five minutes. California Rolls (page 112) are the classic rolled entrée, but Garden Wraps (page 111) and Spring Rolls (page 117) are also delicious. Raw entrées can be served either alone or with a vegetable side dish (see pages 123-132).

# Garden Wraps

Yield: 1 serving

6 thin slices onion
1/2 cup thinly sliced mushrooms
1 tablespoon tamari
1 large collard leaf
1/2 ripe avocado, sliced
1/4 cucumber, seeded and cut lengthwise into thin
  strips
1/4 cup grated carrot or carrot ribbons (see Tools
  and Techniques, page 21)

Place the onion, mushrooms, and tamari in a medium mixing bowl and toss. Work the tamari into the vegetables using a rubber spatula or your hands. Marinate for 10 minutes. Drain off any excess tamari. Cut off the thickest part of the collard leaf stem. Lay the collard leaf horizontally on the cutting board, with the inside facing up. Layer the onions and mushrooms, avocado, cucumber, and carrot on the leaf. Roll up the leaf burrito style, tucking in the ends as you go. Slice the roll into two pieces. Serve immediately.

See photo facing page 121

*Thanks to Alissa Cohen for this collard roll-up recipe. Collard greens make colorful wrappers in this nutrition-packed entrée.*

## Equipment

peeler
cutting board
chef's knife, 8-inch
mandoline (optional)
grater
measuring cups
measuring spoons
medium mixing bowl
rubber spatula

# California Rolls

*See photo facing page 80*

*With a little practice, you'll be rolling sushi like a pro. California Rolls make stunning appetizers at any party, as well as satisfying sandwich substitutes in lunch boxes.*

## Equipment

peeler

cutting board

chef's knife, 8-inch

grater

bamboo sushi mat

measuring cups

measuring spoons

small bowl with water, for sealing the roll

serrated knife, 5-inch

plate

small bowl for serving tamari (optional)

Yield: 2 rolls, 1 serving

2 nori sheets

2 teaspoons mellow white miso

2 cups alfalfa or clover sprouts

$1/2$ ripe avocado, thinly sliced

$1/4$ cucumber, seeded and cut lengthwise into thin strips

$1/4$ cup grated carrot or carrot ribbons (see Tools and Techniques, page 21)

$1/4$ red bell pepper, cut lengthwise into thin strips

Tamari for dipping (optional)

Lay one sheet of nori, shiny side down, on a bamboo sushi mat. Using the back of a teaspoon, spread 1 teaspoon of the miso in a single horizontal strip anywhere along the bottom third of the nori. Along the edge of the nori closest to you, layer the sprouts, avocado, cucumber, carrot, and bell pepper.

To roll, grip the edges of the nori sheet and the sushi mat together with your thumbs and forefingers, and press the filling back toward you with your other fingers. Using the mat to help you, roll the front edge of the nori over the filling. Squeeze it with the mat; then lift the mat and continue rolling.

Just before completing the roll, dip your index finger in water and run it along the far edge of the nori sheet. This will seal the seam of the roll. Cut the roll into 6 pieces with a serrated knife. Fill, roll, and slice the other sheet of nori the same way. Arrange on a plate and serve immediately, with a small bowl of tamari for dipping, if desired.

## Variation

• **For Not Tuna Rolls:** Replace the cucumber with ¹/₄ cup Not Tuna Pâté and use 2 tablespoons per roll.

# Avocado Boats

Yield: 1 serving

¹/₂ ripe avocado, pit removed
¹/₄ cup diced ripe mango or Salsa (page 69)
Dash salt
¹/₄ teaspoon fresh lime juice

Equipment
cutting board
chef's knife, 8-inch
plate
spoon

Peel the avocado half (see Tools and Techniques, page 22). Use a teaspoon to remove a small amount of the avocado meat to create a cavity for stuffing. Fill with the mango and sprinkle with the salt and lime juice. Serve immediately.

# Lasagne

This wheat-free lasagne is rich in authentic Italian flavor. Strips of zucchini replace the noodles, and avocado replaces the cheese.

## Equipment

cutting board

chef's knife, 8-inch

measuring cups

measuring spoons

small mixing bowl

rubber spatula

peeler

mandoline (optional)

food processor

small square container (such as a plastic container used for leftovers)

Yield: 1 to 2 servings

$1/2$ zucchini, peeled

2 cups spinach leaves, tightly packed

$1/2$ cup Marinara Sauce (page 65)

$1/2$ ripe avocado, mashed

Thinly slice the zucchini lengthwise into long, wide noodles using a mandoline or a sharp knife. Place the spinach in a food processor fitted with the S blade and pulse or process until finely chopped. Transfer to a medium bowl.

Coat the bottom of a small square container with 2 tablespoons of the Marinara Sauce and arrange a third of the zucchini noodles in a layer over it. Top with 2 tablespoons of the Marinara Sauce. Add a layer of half of the avocado. Top with half of the spinach and press with the rubber spatula. Repeat this layering process. A third of the zucchini and 2 tablespoons of the Marinara Sauce should remain. Layer the zucchini on top and cover with the Marinara.

Stored in a sealed container in the refrigerator, Lasagne will keep for two days.

## Variation

- **For Lasagne with Cheese:** Replace the avocado with
1/4 cup soft goat cheese or ricotta.

# Not Meat Balls

Yield: 1 serving

1/2 cup Walnut Pâté (page 71)
2 tablespoons Marinara Sauce (page 65)

Form the pâté into 2 or 3 balls and place on a serving plate. Cover each ball with a thin coating of the Marinara Sauce and serve immediately.

*See photo facing page 120*

*Serve plain or with Zucchini Noodles Marinara (page 120) for an Italian dinner.*

## Equipment

serving plate
spoon

# Mock Rice Pilaf

*Grated zucchini replaces rice in this savory Middle Eastern dish.*

## Equipment

peeler

chef's knife, 8-inch

cutting board

grater, or a food processor fitted with a shredding disk

measuring cups

measuring spoons

small mixing bowl

rubber spatula

Yield: 1 serving

1 cup peeled and grated zucchini (about 1 zucchini)

1/8 teaspoon salt

3 tablespoons Marinara Sauce (page 65)

1 tablespoon chopped raw pine nuts

2 teaspoons dark or golden raisins, soaked 10 minutes and drained

1 teaspoon minced fresh parsley or dill weed

Place the zucchini and salt in a mixing bowl, toss, and let rest 5 minutes. Squeeze out the liquid with your hands and discard. Add the Marinara Sauce, pine nuts, raisins, and parsley to the zucchini and toss gently. Serve immediately.

# Spring Rolls

Yield: 1 serving

1 savoy or napa cabbage leaf (see note)

$1/2$ cup mung bean sprouts or shredded lettuce

$1/4$ cup grated carrot or carrot ribbons (see Tools and Techniques, page 21)

$1/4$ cucumber, made into ribbons (see Tools and Techniques, page 21)

2 cilantro sprigs, or 2 fresh mint leaves

$1 1/2$ tablespoons Mock Peanut Sauce (page 66) plus extra for dipping

Cut off the thickest part of the cabbage leaf stem. Lay the leaf horizontally on the cutting board, with the inside facing up. Layer the sprouts, carrot, cucumber, and cilantro on the leaf. Drizzle with the Mock Peanut Sauce. Roll up the leaf, tucking in the ends as you go. Slice the roll into two pieces. Serve immediately.

Note: Savoy and napa cabbage leaves are soft and roll easily.

## Variation

• For Vegetables with Mock Peanut Sauce: Omit the cabbage leaf. Toss the vegetables with the Mock Peanut Sauce and serve immediately.

*Spring rolls make a delicious centerpiece to any Asian-themed meal. For a more traditional roll, replace the cabbage leaf with a piece of rice paper dipped in water. Serve with Miso Soup (page 81).*

## Equipment

cutting board
chef's knife, 8-inch
measuring cups
measuring spoons
grater

# Stuffed Mushrooms

See photo facing page 40

## Equipment

cutting board
chef's knife, 8-inch
teaspoon
measuring cups
measuring spoons
medium mixing bowl
plate
rubber spatula

Yield: 1 serving

1 portobello mushroom
2 teaspoons tamari
1/4 cup Sunflower Herb Pâté or Sunflower
   Sun-dried Tomato Pâté (page 72)
1/2 teaspoon minced fresh parsley, for garnish
   (optional)

Cut the stem from the mushroom. Use a teaspoon to remove enough of the inside of the mushroom cap to create a cavity for stuffing. Place the cap in a mixing bowl, sprinkle with the tamari, and toss until the cap is coated. Marinate for 5 to 30 minutes.

Place the mushroom cap on a plate, with the inside of the cap facing up. Stuff with the pâté and garnish with the parsley, if desired. Serve immediately.

## Variation

• **For Appetizer Stuffed Mushrooms:** Replace the portobello mushroom with 8 small mushrooms. Stuff each mushroom with 1 1/2 teaspoons of pâté. Yield: 4 servings.

# Tomato Stacks

Yield: 1 serving

2 slices large ripe tomato
¼ cup Walnut Pâté (page 71), Not Tuna Pâté
    (page 68), or Pesto (page 70)
2 tablespoons alfalfa or clover sprouts
1 teaspoon sliced black olives

Place one tomato slice on a plate and spread 2 tablespoons of
the pâté over it. Place the second tomato slice on top, and
spread with the remaining 2 tablespoons of pâté. Top with the
alfalfa sprouts and black olives. Serve immediately.

*Juicy tomatoes complement a
rich pâté or pesto perfectly.
Serve with a knife and fork
for easy eating.*

## Equipment

cutting board
serrated knife, 5-inch
measuring cups
measuring spoons
plate

# Zucchini Pasta al Pesto

*See photo facing this page*

*You won't miss wheat pasta in this flavorful Italian entrée. For an elegant presentation, serve it in a shallow bowl.*

## Equipment

peeler
cutting board
chef's knife, 8-inch
vegetable spiral slicer
measuring cups
medium mixing bowl
tongs

Yield: 1 serving

1 zucchini, peeled
2 tablespoons Pesto (page 70)

Cut the zucchini into thin noodles using a vegetable spiral slicer. Alternatively, use a vegetable peeler to create long ribbons, or "fettuccine," by drawing the peeler down all sides of the zucchini until you reach the core. Place in a medium bowl and toss with the pesto. Serve immediately.

Note: To serve warm, heat the sauce gently on the stove for a minute, taking care not to overheat it. Toss with the pasta and serve immediately.

## Variations

• **For Zucchini Pasta with Marinara or Puttanesca Sauce:** Replace the Pesto with 2 tablespoons Marinara Sauce or Puttanesca Sauce (page 65).

• **For Thai Zucchini Noodles:** Replace the Pesto with 2 tablespoons Mock Peanut Sauce (page 66).

• **For Zucchini Fettuccine Alfredo:** Toss the zucchini ribbons with 2 tablespoons Ranch Dressing (page 104).

*Zucchini Pasta with Marinara Sauce, above, page 65, and Not Meat Balls, page 115*

# Stuffed Bell Peppers

Yield: 1 serving

$1/2$ red bell pepper, seeded (or $1/4$ red bell pepper, if large)

$1/4$ cup Not Tuna Pâté (page 68), Sunflower Herb Pâté (page 72), or Guacamole (page 63)

$1/2$ teaspoon minced fresh parsley, for garnish (optional)

**Equipment**

cutting board
chef's knife, 8-inch
paring knife
tablespoon

Trim the white membranes from the pepper using a paring knife. Fill the pepper with the pâté and garnish with the parsley, if desired. Serve immediately.

## Variation

• **For Stuffed Tomatoes:** Replace the red bell pepper half with a whole ripe tomato. To prepare the tomato for stuffing, cut out the section around the stem with a paring knife, and remove. Insert a small measuring spoon into the hole and scoop out the seeds and membranes of the tomato. Stuff with the pâté and garnish with the parsley, if desired.

*Garden Wraps, page 111*

# *V*egetable *S*ide *D*ishes

To make raw vegetables—such as beets, broccoli, cabbage, carrots, cauliflower, collard greens and kale—more palatable, marinate them in a dressing of extra-virgin olive oil, lemon juice, and salt. This breaks down the fibers, just like cooking does, but without the loss of nutrients and flavors. When you marinate kale or collard greens, work the dressing into them with your hands. Also, the finer you slice, shred, or chop the vegetables, the more easily the marinade can penetrate and soften them.

# Cucumbers with Fresh Mint

Yield: 1 serving

1 cup Pressed Cucumbers (page 31)
1 tablespoon minced fresh mint
1 1/2 teaspoons extra-virgin olive oil
1 teaspoon fresh lemon juice
1/4 teaspoon crushed garlic (1/2 clove)
Dash ground cumin
Dash black pepper

Place all the ingredients in a mixing bowl and toss. Stored in a sealed container in the refrigerator, Cucumbers with Fresh Mint will keep for three days.

*This dish makes a nice accompaniment to California Rolls (page 112) or Not Tuna Rolls (page 113).*

## Equipment

cutting board
chef's knife, 8-inch
measuring cups
measuring spoons
citrus juicer or reamer
garlic press
medium mixing bowl
rubber spatula

# Carrots with Moroccan Spices

See photo facing page 40.

This dish complements Mock Rice Pilaf (page 116) nicely.

## Equipment

cutting board
chef's knife, 8-inch
mandoline (optional)
citrus juicer or reamer
measuring cups
measuring spoons
medium mixing bowl
rubber spatula

Yield: 1 cup, 1 to 2 servings

2 carrots, peeled
2 tablespoons chopped fresh parsley
2 tablespoons fresh orange juice
1 1/2 teaspoons fresh lemon juice
1 1/2 teaspoons extra-virgin olive oil
1/8 teaspoon salt
Dash cayenne
Dash ground cinnamon
Dash ground cumin
Dash black pepper

Thinly slice the carrots using a mandoline or a sharp knife. Place in a mixing bowl along with the remaining ingredients. Toss well. Stored in a sealed container in the refrigerator, Carrots with Moroccan Spices will keep for three days.

# Carrots with Parsley and Walnuts

Yield: 1 cup, 1 serving

2 carrots, grated (about 1 cup)
2 tablespoons chopped fresh parsley
2 tablespoons chopped raw walnuts, unsoaked
2 teaspoons fresh lemon juice
2 teaspoons extra-virgin olive oil
1/8 teaspoon salt
Dash black pepper (optional)

Equipment

cutting board
peeler
chef's knife, 8-inch
grater, or a food
processor fitted with a
shredding disk
measuring cups
measuring spoons
citrus juicer or reamer
medium mixing bowl
rubber spatula

Place all the ingredients in a mixing bowl and toss well. Stored in a sealed container in the refrigerator, Carrots with Parsley and Walnuts will keep for three days.

## Variation

• For Carrots with Golden Raisins and Mint: Omit the parsley and walnuts. Add 2 tablespoons golden raisins, soaked 10 minutes (to plump and soften them) and drained, and 2 tablespoons chopped fresh mint.

# Coleslaw

This sweet-and-sour slaw is a delightful change from typical mayonnaise-laden coleslaw.

## Equipment

cutting board

peeler

chef's knife, 8-inch

mandoline (optional)

grater, or food processor fitted with a shredding disk

measuring cups

measuring spoons

mixing bowl

rubber spatula

Yield: 1 1/2 cups, 1 serving

1 cup Pressed Cabbage (page 31)

1/2 carrot, grated (about 1/4 cup)

1/4 cup thinly sliced red onion (optional)

2 tablespoons extra-virgin olive oil

1 tablespoon apple cider vinegar or fresh lemon juice

1 1/2 teaspoons raw honey or agave nectar

1/4 teaspoon whole celery seeds (optional)

Dash black pepper

Place all the ingredients in a mixing bowl and toss well. Stored in a sealed container in the refrigerator, Coleslaw will keep for three days.

Note: To thinly slice the onion, use a mandoline or a sharp knife.

# Latin American Cabbage

Yield: 2 cups, 1 serving

1 cup Pressed Cabbage (page 31)
1/2 ripe tomato, seeded and diced
1/4 cucumber, peeled, seeded, and thinly sliced
1/2 celery stalk, diced
1/4 red bell pepper, diced
2 tablespoons minced fresh cilantro
1 tablespoon fresh lime juice
2 teaspoons minced onion
1 1/2 teaspoons extra-virgin olive oil

Place all the ingredients in a mixing bowl and toss well. Marinate for 10 minutes at room temperature before serving. Stored in a sealed container in the refrigerator, Latin American Cabbage will keep for two days.

Note: To thinly slice the cucumber, use a mandoline or a sharp knife.

*This authentic Costa Rican dish tastes delicious with Guacamole (page 63) and Papaya Lime Soup (page 82).*

## Equipment

mandoline (optional)
cutting board
serrated knife, 5-inch
chef's knife, 8-inch
citrus juicer or reamer
measuring spoons
medium mixing bowl
tongs

# Mediterranean Kale

See photo facing page 40.

*When kale is cut into thin strips and marinated in a dressing, it develops a soft and juicy texture.*

## Equipment

cutting board
chef's knife, 8-inch
measuring spoons
medium mixing bowl
citrus juicer or reamer
serrated knife, 5-inch
tongs

Yield: 1 serving

4 kale leaves, stems removed
1½ teaspoons extra-virgin olive oil
1½ teaspoons fresh lemon juice
⅛ teaspoon salt
¼ red bell pepper, diced
1 tablespoon raw pine nuts
1 tablespoon sliced black olives
Dash black pepper (optional)

Stack 2 of the kale leaves with the stem end facing you. Fold in half lengthwise and roll tightly like a cigar. Slice crosswise into thin strips. Repeat with the remaining 2 leaves. Chop the kale strips crosswise a few times, so they aren't too long. Place in a mixing bowl along with the olive oil, lemon juice, and salt. Toss well with your hands, working the dressing into the greens. Add the red bell pepper, pine nuts, and olives and toss gently. Marinate for 10 minutes at room temperature before serving. Season to taste with black pepper, if desired. Stored in a sealed container in the refrigerator, Mediterranean Kale will keep for three days. Bring to room temperature before serving.

## Variations

• **For Mediterranean Kale with Pine Nuts and Raisins:** Omit the red bell pepper and olives. Add 1 tablespoon golden raisins.

• **For Mediterranean Parsley:** Replace the kale with ¾ cup minced fresh parsley. You do not need to work the dressing into the parsley with your hands; just toss everything together with a rubber spatula.

# Marinated Vegetables

Yield: 1 serving

1 cup small broccoli florets
6 cremini mushrooms, quartered
½ cup thinly sliced carrot (½ carrot)
3 tablespoons Lemon Herb Dressing (page 102) or
   Classic Vinaigrette (page 99)

Place all the ingredients in a mixing bowl. Toss well with your hands, working the dressing into the vegetables. Marinate for 4 to 12 hours in the refrigerator before serving. Stored in a sealed container in the refrigerator, Marinated Vegetables will keep for three days. Bring to room temperature before serving.

*Marinating broccoli and mushrooms makes them taste like they were cooked— without the loss of nutrients.*

## Equipment

cutting board
chef's knife, 8-inch
peeler
measuring cups
medium mixing bowl
rubber spatula
strainer
salad spinner
tongs

# Southern Greens

## Equipment

cutting board
chef's knife, 8-inch
measuring spoons
garlic press
medium mixing bowl

Yield: 1 serving

4 curly green or red kale leaves, or a mixture, stems removed
2 collard leaves, stems removed
4 fresh basil leaves, chopped
2 teaspoons extra-virgin olive oil
2 teaspoons fresh lemon juice
$\frac{1}{2}$ teaspoon garlic, crushed (1 clove)
$\frac{1}{8}$ teaspoon salt
Dash cayenne

Chop the kale medium-fine and transfer to a mixing bowl. To prepare the collards, first stack the leaves with the stem end facing you. Fold in half lengthwise and roll tightly like a cigar. Slice into thin strips, then chop medium-fine. Place in the bowl with the kale and add the basil, olive oil, lemon juice, garlic, salt, and cayenne. Work the dressing into the greens with your hands. Marinate for 10 minutes at room temperature before serving. Stored in a sealed container in the refrigerator, Southern Greens will keep for three days. Bring to room temperature before serving.

## Variations

• For Indian Greens: Replace the collard greens with 2 leaves of mustard greens. Omit the basil and add a dash of curry powder and a dash of ground cumin.

• For Asian Greens: Replace the collard greens with 2 stalks of bok choy. Omit the basil and salt and add $\frac{1}{2}$ teaspoon tamari and $\frac{1}{4}$ teaspoon grated fresh ginger.

# Tabouli

Yield: 1 serving

³/₄ cup minced fresh parsley
1 tablespoon minced fresh mint
¹/₂ Roma tomato, seeded and diced
1 tablespoon chopped green onion
1¹/₂ teaspoons fresh lemon juice
1¹/₂ teaspoons extra-virgin olive oil
¹/₈ teaspoon salt

*My raw tabouli is lighter than the traditional bulgur wheat version of this fragrant Middle Eastern dish.*

## Equipment

cutting board
chef's knife, 8-inch
measuring cups
measuring spoons
serrated knife, 5-inch
citrus juicer or reamer
small mixing bowl
rubber spatula

Place all the ingredients in a mixing bowl and toss well. Stored in a sealed container in the refrigerator, Tabouli will keep for three days.

# Swiss Chard with Pine Nuts and Raisins

*This elegant Italian preparation tastes like a cooked side dish you'd order at a fine Italian restaurant.*

## Equipment

cutting board
chef's knife, 8-inch
measuring spoons
medium mixing bowl

Yield: 1 serving

4 Swiss chard leaves, stems removed
1 1/2 teaspoons extra-virgin olive oil
1 1/2 teaspoons fresh lemon juice
1/8 teaspoon salt
1 tablespoon raw pine nuts
1 tablespoon golden raisins, soaked 10 minutes
  and drained
Dash black pepper (optional)

Stack 2 of the chard leaves with the stem end facing you. Fold in half lengthwise and roll tightly like a cigar. Slice crosswise into thin strips. Repeat with the remaining 2 leaves. Chop the chard strips crosswise a few times, so they aren't too long. Place in a mixing bowl and add the olive oil, lemon juice, and salt. Toss well with your hands, working the dressing into the greens. Add the pine nuts and raisins and toss gently. Season with black pepper, if desired. Marinate for 10 minutes at room temperature before serving. Stored in a sealed container in the refrigerator, Swiss Chard with Pine Nuts and Raisins will keep for three days. Bring to room temperature before serving.

# Dessert

Any dessert that you enjoy cooked—cake, cookies, fruit crisps, pies, tarts, puddings, mousses, shakes, and ice creams—can be made raw. Raw desserts use whole food ingredients such as nuts, dried fruits, and avocados to replace unhealthful white flour, white sugar, and heated fats. Try Chocolate Mousse (page 160) for an elegant end to lunch or dinner, Almond Cookies (page 140) or Brownies (page 142) with Almond Milk (page 28) as an afternoon snack, or a piece of Tropical Fruit Tart (page 156) as a light meal itself. Most of the recipes in this section provide more than two servings, which makes them perfect for sharing with friends.

# Cakes, Cookies, and Bars

Raw cakes, cookies, and bars are made from nuts, dried fruits, and flavorings such as cocoa, carob, citrus zest, and extracts. For the best texture, use unsoaked dried fruits and unsoaked nuts. There's no need for cake pans or cookie sheets—these delicious no-bake desserts require only a food processor. To make a larger cake or batch of cookies, just double or triple the recipe.

# Walnut-Raisin Cake

*This rich, fudgy cake couldn't be easier, yet it's elegant enough to serve at any party. Thank you to Alissa Cohen for inspiring this recipe with her Date-Nut Torte.*

## Equipment

measuring cups
food processor
rubber spatula
serving plate

Yield: one 5-inch cake, 4 servings

1 cup raw walnuts, unsoaked
1 cup raisins, unsoaked
1/4 cup Lemon Glaze or Orange Glaze (page 162)
1/2 cup fresh raspberries

Place the walnuts and raisins in a food processor fitted with the S blade and process until the mixture sticks together. Transfer to a serving plate and form into a 5-inch round cake. Frost the top and sides with the glaze. Chill for at least 1 hour. Decorate the cake and plate with fresh raspberries before serving. Covered with plastic wrap, Walnut-Raisin Cake will keep for five days in the refrigerator or two weeks in the freezer. Serve chilled or at room temperature.

Dessert

# Apple Crumb Cake

Yield: one 5-inch cake, 4 servings

3/4 cup dried apples, tightly packed, unsoaked
3 pitted medjool dates, unsoaked
I apple, peeled and grated
1/8 teaspoon ground cinnamon
I cup Crumble Topping (page 144)
2 tablespoons Vanilla Crème Sauce (page 166) or
   Sweet Orange Cream Sauce (page 164;
   optional)

*This moist, scrumptious "coffee cake" has a crumble topping and a drizzle of white icing.*

## Equipment

measuring cups
measuring spoons
cutting board
peeler
chef's knife, 8-inch
grater, or food processor fitted with a coarse shredding disk
food processor
rubber spatula
serving plate

Place the dried apples in a food processor fitted with the S blade and process until ground. Add the dates and process until finely chopped. Add the grated apple and cinnamon and process until well combined. Stop occasionally to scrape down the sides of the bowl with a rubber spatula.

Place 1/2 cup of the Crumble Topping on a serving plate, and shape it into a 5-inch round crust. Put the apple mixture on top, and form it into a cake, following the edges of the crust. Place the remaining Crumble Topping on the top and around the sides of the cake. Chill for at least I hour. Drizzle with the Vanilla Crème Sauce before serving, if desired. Covered with plastic wrap in the refrigerator, Apple Crumb Cake will keep for three days. Bring to room temperature before serving.

# Spanish Fig Cake

*This Spanish confection is traditionally served in thin wedges with cheese and fruit for a snack or dessert.*

## Equipment

cutting board
paring knife
measuring cups
food processor
rubber spatula
serving plate

Yield: one 5-inch cake, 4 servings

$^3/_4$ cup Black Mission or Calimyrna figs
$^1/_2$ cup raw almonds, unsoaked
$^1/_4$ cup raw walnuts, unsoaked
$^1/_2$ cup mixed fresh berries (blueberries, blackberries, or raspberries; optional)

If the figs are dry, soak them for 10 minutes and drain. Trim off the stems with a paring knife. Place the almonds and walnuts in a food processor fitted with the S blade and process until coarsely chopped. Add the figs and process until the mixture sticks together. Transfer to a serving plate and form into a 5-inch round cake. Decorate the cake and plate with fresh berries before serving, if desired. Covered with plastic wrap, Spanish Fig Cake will keep for three days in the refrigerator or two weeks in the freezer. Bring to room temperature before serving.

## Variation

- **For Spanish Date Cake:** Replace the figs with pitted, unsoaked medjool dates.

# Not Peanut Butter Cookies

Yield: 8 cookies, 4 servings

1/2 cup raw almond or cashew butter
1/4 cup pure maple syrup, agave nectar,
   or raw honey
1/2 teaspoon vanilla extract
Dash salt
1/2 cup ground almonds (page 30)

Place the almond butter, maple syrup, vanilla, and salt in a food processor fitted with the S blade and process until smooth. Transfer to a small bowl and freeze for 30 minutes. Form into 1-inch balls and flatten slightly. Roll each cookie in the ground almonds. Freeze for at least 2 hours before serving. Stored in a sealed container in the freezer, Not Peanut Butter Cookies will keep for up to one month.

*My raw "peanut butter" cookies use almond or cashew butter.*

## Equipment

measuring cups
measuring spoons
food processor
rubber spatula
small mixing bowl

# Flourless Chocolate Cake

See photo facing page 161

*This decadent dessert will delight chocolate lovers.*

## Equipment

measuring cups
measuring spoons
food processor
rubber spatula
small mixing bowl
serving plate

Yield: one 5-inch cake, 4 servings

1 1/2 cups raw walnuts, unsoaked
Dash salt
8 pitted medjool dates, unsoaked
1/3 cup unsweetened cocoa or carob powder
1/2 teaspoon vanilla extract (optional)
2 teaspoons water
1/2 cup fresh raspberries, for garnish (optional)

Place the walnuts and salt in a food processor fitted with the S blade and process until finely ground. Add the dates, cocoa powder, and optional vanilla and process until the mixture begins to stick together. Add the water and process briefly.

Transfer to a serving plate and form into a 5-inch round cake. Decorate the cake and plate with fresh raspberries before serving, if desired. Covered with plastic wrap, Flourless Chocolate Cake will keep for three days in the refrigerator or two weeks in the freezer. Bring to room temperature before serving.

# Variations

• **For Chocolate Cake with Raspberry Sauce:** Serve each slice of cake with 1 tablespoon Raspberry Sauce (page 165).

• **For Black Forest Cake:** Top the cake with ¾ cup pitted fresh or frozen cherries (thaw and drain, if frozen). Drizzle with 2 tablespoons Vanilla Crème Sauce (page 166).

• **For Chocolate Layer Cake with Raspberry Filling and Chocolate Buttercream Frosting:** Double the recipe to make 2 (5-inch) cakes. Frost the top of one cake with ¼ cup Raspberry Sauce (page 165). Place the other cake on top and frost the top and sides with ½ cup Chocolate Buttercream Frosting (page 161). Chill for at least 1 hour before serving. Yield: 6 to 8 servings.

# Almond Cookies

*This mixture tastes so good that you may wish to skip forming the dough into cookies and eat it straight out of the bowl!*

## Equipment

measuring cups
measuring spoons
food processor
small mixing bowl
rubber spatula
serving plate

Yield: 12 cookies, 4 servings

$^1/_2$ cup raw almonds, unsoaked
$^1/_4$ cup raw walnuts, unsoaked
Dash salt
$^1/_2$ cup pitted medjool dates, unsoaked
$^1/_4$ teaspoon almond extract
$^1/_4$ cup raisins or dried cherries, unsoaked (optional)
$^1/_4$ cup ground almonds (page 30)

Place the almonds, walnuts, and salt in a food processor fitted with the S blade and process until coarsely chopped. Add the dates and almond extract and process until the mixture begins to stick together. Don't overprocess; you should still see chunks of almonds and walnuts. Add the raisins, if desired, and pulse briefly, just to mix. Remove from the food processor and place in a small mixing bowl.

Scoop about 1 tablespoon of the almond mixture into your hand and squeeze firmly until it sticks together. Roll into a 1-inch ball and flatten slightly, to make a cookie. Repeat until you have used up all the almond mixture. Roll each cookie in the ground almonds, and place on a plate. Chill at least 1 hour before serving. Stored in a sealed container, Almond Cookies will keep for up to one month in the refrigerator or three months in the freezer.

# Variations

• **For Chocolate Chip Cookies:** Replace the raisins with chocolate or carob chips, and add 1 teaspoon orange zest, if desired. Although these cookies aren't totally raw, they are much healthier than the traditional version.

• **For Schoolboy Cookies:** Omit the raisins and press a small square of dark chocolate onto the top of each cookie.

• **For Lemon Cookies:** Replace the almond extract with lemon extract and add 1 teaspoon lemon zest.

# Brownies

*Thank you to raw food chef Elaina Love for this recipe, which was adapted from her Black Forest Cherry Brownies.*

## Equipment

measuring cups

measuring spoons

food processor

rubber spatula

small mixing bowl

small square container (such as a plastic container used for leftovers)

Yield: 8 brownies, 4 servings

1½ cups raw walnuts, unsoaked

Dash salt

8 pitted medjool dates, unsoaked

⅓ cup unsweetened cocoa or carob powder

½ teaspoon vanilla or cherry extract (optional)

2 teaspoons water (for a moister brownie; optional)

¼ cup chopped dried cherries (optional)

Chop ¼ cup of the walnuts and set aside. Place the remaining walnuts and the salt in a food processor fitted with the S blade and process until finely ground. Add the dates and process until the mixture sticks together. Add the cocoa powder and optional vanilla and process until evenly distributed. Add the water, if using, and process briefly.

Transfer to a mixing bowl. Add the reserved chopped walnuts and dried cherries, if desired, and mix well using your hands. Pack the mixture firmly into a square container. Stored in a sealed container, Brownies will keep for up to one week in the refrigerator or one month in the freezer.

## Variation

• For Chocolate Chip Brownies: Replace the dried cherries with chocolate chips. Although these brownies aren't totally raw, they are much healthier than the traditional version.

# Crisps, Pies, and Tarts

Raw pie and tart crusts are made from nuts, coconut, and salt, which lend a buttery taste, plus dates, which bind the crust ingredients together. Crisps are made with Crumble Topping (page 144), a sweet mixture of ground nuts, dates, raisins, and spices. Fruit fillings for these desserts use fresh and dried fruits; creamy fillings use avocados (but once you add flavorings, such as agave nectar, lime juice, or cocoa, no one will know). To make a tart instead of a pie, use a tart pan with a removable bottom. Once you have filled the crust, push up on the bottom to release the tart from the pan.

Raw pie and tart dough is not rolled out; it is shaped with your hands. To form the crust, simply pour the crumbly dough into the pan. Use a light circular motion with your palm and fingers to distribute the crumbs uniformly along the bottom and up the sides of the pan. There should be a ¾-inch lip of crumbs along the sides. After the crumbs are evenly distributed, press the crust down on the bottom of the pan using your fingers and palm. Be sure to press especially firmly where the bottom of the pan joins the sides. Then press the crust against the pan's sides, shaping it so that its edges are flush with the rim.

The recipes in this section provide standard-size crisps, pies, and tarts that are enough for eight servings, but you can make individual-size crisps and tarts instead. Just divide any crust and filling recipe in half, and use ramekins or small bowls for individual-size crisps, and five-inch tart pans for miniature tarts. You can freeze any leftover crust for future use, and eat extra fruit fillings for breakfasts and snacks.

# Crumble Topping

*This topping tastes like it was freshly baked! Use it on crisps, as a crust for Apple Crumb Cake (page 135), or eat it straight.*

## Equipment

measuring cups
measuring spoons
food processor
rubber spatula

Yield: 2 cups, 8 servings

2 cups raw walnuts or pecans, unsoaked
1/2 cup unsweetened shredded dried coconut
1/4 teaspoon ground cinnamon
1/4 teaspoon ground nutmeg
1/4 teaspoon salt
1/2 cup raisins, unsoaked
8 pitted medjool dates, unsoaked
1/4 cup whole cane sugar or maple sugar
    (optional, for a sweeter topping)

Place the walnuts, coconut, cinnamon, nutmeg, and salt in a food processor fitted with the S blade and process until coarsely ground. Add the raisins and dates and process until the mixture resembles coarse crumbs and begins to stick together. Don't overprocess. Add the optional whole cane sugar and process briefly. Stored in a sealed container, Crumble Topping will keep for one month in the refrigerator or three months in the freezer.

# Coconut Crust

Yield: 3 cups, for one 9-inch pie or tart crust

1½ cups unsweetened shredded dried coconut
1½ cups raw macadamia nuts or raw walnuts, unsoaked
½ teaspoon salt
½ cup pitted medjool dates, unsoaked

Place the coconut, macadamia nuts or walnuts, and salt in a food processor fitted with the S blade and process until coarsely ground. Add the dates and process until the mixture resembles coarse crumbs and begins to stick together. Don't overprocess. Stored in a sealed container, Coconut Crust will keep for one month in the refrigerator or three months in the freezer.

*See photo facing page 160*

*The perfect crust for Key Lime Tart (page 150) and Tropical Fruit Tart (page 156). Thanks to raw food chef Matt Samuelson for this recipe.*

## Equipment

measuring cups
measuring spoons
food processor
rubber spatula

# Fig Crust

Yield: 3 cups, for one 9-inch pie or tart crust

1⅓ cups Black Mission figs
2 cups raw pecans, unsoaked

If the figs are dry, soak them for 10 minutes and drain. Trim off the stems with a paring knife. Place the figs and pecans in a food processor fitted with the S blade and process until the mixture sticks together. Stored in a sealed container, Fig Crust will keep for two weeks in the refrigerator or one month in the freezer.

## Equipment

measuring cups
cutting board
paring knife
food processor
rubber spatula

# Almond Crust

This delicately flavored crust goes well with any pie or tart filling.

## Equipment

measuring cups
measuring spoons
food processor
rubber spatula

Yield: 3 cups, for one 9-inch pie or tart crust

2 $\frac{1}{4}$ cups ground almonds (page 30)
$\frac{3}{4}$ cup pitted medjool dates, unsoaked
$\frac{1}{4}$ teaspoon salt

Place all the ingredients in a food processor fitted with the S blade and process until the mixture resembles coarse crumbs and begins to stick together. Don't overprocess. Stored in a sealed container, Almond Crust will keep for one month in the refrigerator or three months in the freezer.

# Walnut Crust

## Equipment

measuring cups
measuring spoons
food processor
rubber spatula

Yield: 3 cups, for one 9-inch pie or tart crust

2 cups raw walnuts, unsoaked
I cup unsweetened shredded dried coconut
$\frac{1}{4}$ teaspoon salt
$\frac{1}{2}$ cup pitted medjool dates, unsoaked

Place the walnuts, coconut, and salt in a food processor fitted with the S blade and process until coarsely ground. Add the dates and process until the mixture resembles coarse crumbs and begins to stick together. Don't overprocess. Stored in a sealed container, Walnut Crust will keep for one month in the refrigerator or three months in the freezer.

# Apple Crisp

Yield: one 8-inch crisp, 8 servings

2 apples, peeled and thinly sliced
3 tablespoons fresh lemon juice
2 apples, peeled and chopped
½ cup pitted medjool dates, soaked
½ cup raisins, soaked
¼ teaspoon ground cinnamon
2 cups Crumble Topping (page 144)

*Serve plain or with Vanilla Crème Sauce (page 166) or Vanilla Ice Cream (page 169).*

## Equipment

cutting board
peeler
chef's knife, 8-inch
paring knife
measuring cups
measuring spoons
food processor
rubber spatula
small mixing bowl
square glass pan, 8-inch

Toss the sliced apples with 2 tablespoons of the lemon juice and set aside. Place the chopped apples, dates, raisins, cinnamon, and remaining 1 tablespoon of lemon juice in a food processor fitted with the S blade and process until smooth. Remove from the food processor and mix with the sliced apples.

To assemble the crisp, press ½ cup of the Crumble Topping into an 8-inch square glass baking dish. Spread the apple filling on top using a rubber spatula. Using your hands, knead pieces of the remaining 1 ½ cups of Crumble Topping until they stick together. Lay these pieces of topping on the apple filling to form a cobbled appearance, allowing some of the filling to peek through. Serve at room temperature, or warm in a slow oven or dehydrator (see note). Covered with plastic wrap in the refrigerator, Apple Crisp will keep for three days.

**Note:** To warm, preheat the oven to 200 degrees F. Turn off the oven, insert the Apple Crisp, and warm for 15 minutes. Alternatively, heat the Apple Crisp for 30 minutes in a food dehydrator set at 105 degrees F.

# Blackberry Crisp

## Equipment

cutting board
peeler
chef's knife, 8-inch
paring knife
measuring cups
measuring spoons
food processor
rubber spatula
small mixing bowl
square glass pan, 8-inch

Yield: one 8-inch crisp, 8 servings

4 cups fresh or frozen blackberries (thaw and
   drain, if frozen)
3/4 cup pitted medjool dates, soaked
1 tablespoon fresh lemon juice
2 cups Crumble Topping (page 144)

Place 1 1/2 cups of the blackberries along with the dates and
lemon juice in a food processor fitted with the S blade and
process until smooth. Remove from the food processor and mix
with the remaining blackberries.

To assemble the crisp, press 1/2 cup of the Crumble Topping into
an 8-inch square glass baking dish. Spread the blackberry filling
on top using a rubber spatula. Using your hands, knead pieces of
the remaining 1 1/2 cups of the Crumble Topping until they stick
together. Lay these pieces of topping on the blackberry filling to
form a cobbled appearance, allowing some of the filling to peek
through. Serve at room temperature, or warm in a slow oven or
dehydrator (see note). Covered with plastic wrap in the refrigerator, Blackberry Crisp will keep for three days.

# Variations

• **For Peach Crisp:** Replace the blackberries with an equal amount of chopped peaches. If using frozen peaches, thaw and drain well before chopping. Add $\frac{1}{8}$ teaspoon nutmeg to the filling, if desired.

• **For Blueberry or Cherry Crisp:** Replace the blackberries with an equal amount of fresh or frozen blueberries or pitted cherries (thaw and drain, if frozen).

Note: To warm, preheat the oven to 200 degrees F. Turn off the oven, insert the Blackberry Crisp, and warm for 15 minutes. Alternatively, heat the Blackberry Crisp for 30 minutes in a food dehydrator set at 105 degrees F.

# Key Lime Tart

*The bright green mousse filling and the rainbow rings of fruit make this tart visually stunning as well as delicious.*

## Equipment

measuring cups

pie plate, or tart pan with
   removable bottom, 9-inch

cutting board

paring knife

rubber spatula

Yield: one 9-inch pie or tart

3 cups Coconut Crust (page 145)
2 cups Key Lime Mousse (page 159)
3 kiwifruit, peeled
2 cups fresh raspberries
1 cup fresh blueberries

Scoop the crust into a pie or tart pan. Use a light circular motion with your palm and fingers to distribute the crumbs uniformly along the bottom and up the sides of the pan. There should be a ¾-inch lip of crumbs along the sides. After the crumbs are evenly distributed, press the crust down on the bottom of the pan using your fingers and palm. Be sure to press especially firmly where the bottom of the pan joins the sides. Then press the crust against the pan's sides, shaping it so that the edges are flush with the rim. Place the crust in the freezer for 15 minutes.

Remove the crust from the freezer and spread the Key Lime Mousse over the bottom. Cut the kiwifruit in half lengthwise, then slice them into half-moons. Arrange the slices around the outer edge of the tart, propping them at an angle against the crust. Place the raspberries in front of the kiwifruit slices, creating two or more rings. Mound the blueberries in the center of the tart. Chill for at least 1 hour before serving. Serve chilled or at room temperature.

Covered with plastic wrap in the refrigerator, Key Lime Tart will keep for three days.

## Variation

- **For Lemon Tart:** Replace the Key Lime Mousse with Lemon Mousse (page 159).

- **For Key Lime Sherbet Tart:** After spreading the key lime mousse over the crust, place the tart in the freezer for at least 2 hours. Thaw for 10 minutes before serving. To serve the entire tart, top with the fresh fruit and serve immediately. To serve a portion of the tart, cut individual slices and top each with fresh fruit before serving. Re-freeze the rest of the tart; covered with plastic wrap, it will keep for up to two weeks.

# Apple Pie or Tart

*Dates, raisins, and cinnamon give this pie sweetness and depth.*

## Equipment

measuring cups

measuring spoons

pie plate, or tart pan
with removable
bottom, 9-inch

cutting board

peeler

paring knife

citrus juicer or reamer

food processor

rubber spatula

Yield: one 9-inch pie or tart, 8 servings

3 cups Almond Crust (page 146), Fig Crust
(page 145), or Walnut Crust (page 146)

2 apples, peeled and thinly sliced

3 tablespoons fresh lemon juice

2 apples, peeled and chopped

$1/2$ cup pitted medjool dates, soaked

$1/2$ cup raisins, soaked

$1/4$ teaspoon ground cinnamon

Scoop the crust into a pie plate or tart pan. Use a light circular motion with your palm and fingers to distribute the crumbs uniformly along the bottom and up the sides of the pan. There should be a $3/4$-inch lip of crumbs along the sides. After the crumbs are evenly distributed, press the crust down on the bottom of the pan using your fingers and palm. Be sure to press especially firmly where the bottom of the pan joins the sides. Then press the crust against the pan's sides, shaping it so that its edges are flush with the rim. Place the crust in the freezer for 15 minutes.

Toss the sliced apples with 2 tablespoons of the lemon juice and set aside. Place the chopped apples, dates, raisins, cinnamon, and remaining 1 tablespoon of lemon juice in a food processor fitted with the S blade and process until smooth. Remove from the food processor and mix with the sliced apples.

Remove the crust from the freezer. Pour the apple filling into it and press down with a rubber spatula. Bring to room temperature or warm in a slow oven or dehydrator (see note). Covered with plastic wrap in the refrigerator, Apple Pie or Tart will keep for three days.

## Variation

• **For Apple Cream Pie or Tart:** Pour $3/4$ cup Vanilla Crème Sauce (page 166) onto the crust and smooth with a rubber spatula. Add the apple filling and press with the spatula. Some of the Vanilla Crème Sauce will rise up and mix with the apples. Smooth the entire filling so it is flush with the edge of the crust.

**Note:** To warm, preheat the oven to 200 degrees F. Turn off the oven, insert the Apple Pie or Tart, and warm for 15 minutes. Alternatively, heat the Apple Pie or Tart for 30 minutes in a food dehydrator set at 105 degrees F.

# Blueberry Pie or Tart

## Equipment

measuring cups

measuring spoons

pie plate, or tart pan
   with removable
   bottom, 9-inch

citrus juicer or reamer

blender

rubber spatula

3 cups Almond Crust (page 146) or Walnut Crust
   (page 146)
4 cups fresh or frozen blueberries (thaw and
   drain well, if frozen)
3/4 cup pitted medjool dates, soaked
1 tablespoon fresh lemon juice

Scoop the crust into a pie plate or tart pan. Use a light circular motion with your palm and fingers to distribute the crumbs uniformly along the bottom and up the sides of the pan. There should be a 3/4-inch lip of crumbs along the sides. After the crumbs are evenly distributed, press the crust down on the bottom of the pan using your fingers and palm. Be sure to press especially firmly where the bottom of the pan joins the sides. Then press the crust against the pan's sides, shaping it so that its edges are flush with the rim. Place in the freezer for 15 minutes.

Place 1 1/2 cups of the blueberries along with the dates and lemon juice in a blender, and process until smooth. Transfer to a mixing bowl, add the remaining blueberries, and mix well. Remove the crust from the freezer. Pour the blueberry filling into it and press down with a rubber spatula.

Bring to room temperature or warm in a slow oven or dehydrator (see note). Covered with plastic wrap in the refrigerator, Blueberry Pie or Tart will keep for three days.

## Variations

• **For Peach Pie or Tart:** Replace the blueberries with an equal amount of chopped peaches. If using frozen peaches, thaw and drain well before chopping. Add $\frac{1}{8}$ teaspoon ground nutmeg to the filling, if desired.

• **For Blackberry or Cherry Pie or Tart:** Replace the blueberries with an equal amount of fresh or frozen blackberries or pitted cherries. (Thaw and drain, if frozen.)

**Note:** To warm, preheat the oven to 200 degrees F. Turn off the oven, insert the Blueberry Pie, and warm for 15 minutes. Alternatively, heat the Blueberry Pie for 30 minutes in a food dehydrator set at 105 degrees F.

# Tropical Fruit Tart

See photo facing page 160

*This light, fruity tart is the perfect ending to an Asian or Latin American meal.*

## Equipment

measuring cups

measuring spoons

pie plate, or tart pan with removable bottom, 9-inch

rubber spatula

medium mixing bowl

Yield: one 9-inch pie or tart

3 cups Coconut Crust (page 145)

2 cups Mango Pudding or Pineapple Pudding (page 163)

2 cups fresh raspberries

1 cup fresh blackberries

1 cup fresh blueberries

Scoop the crust into a pie or tart pan. Use a light circular motion with your palm and fingers to distribute the crumbs uniformly along the bottom and up the sides of the pan. There should be a ³/₄-inch lip of crumbs along the sides. After the crumbs are evenly distributed, press the crust down on the bottom of the pan using your fingers and palm. Be sure to press especially firmly where the bottom of the pan joins the sides. Then press the crust against the pan's sides, shaping it so that the edges are flush with the rim. Place the crust in the freezer for 15 minutes.

Remove the crust from the freezer and spread the Mango Pudding over the bottom. Place the berries in a mixing bowl and toss gently. Arrange the berries over the top of the tart so that the entire tart is covered. Chill for at least 1 hour before serving. Serve chilled or at room temperature. Covered with plastic wrap in the refrigerator, Tropical Fruit Tart will keep for three days.

Dessert

# Chocolate Tart with Strawberries

Yield: one 9-inch pie or tart

1 pound fresh strawberries, thinly sliced
3 cups Almond Crust (page 146) or Coconut Crust
   (page 145)
2 cups Chocolate Mousse (page 160)

Scoop the crust into a pie plate or tart pan. Use a light circular motion with your palm and fingers to distribute the crumbs uniformly along the bottom and up the sides of the pan. There should be a 3/4-inch lip of crumbs along the sides. After the crumbs are evenly distributed, press the crust down on the bottom of the pan using your fingers and palm. Be sure that you press especially firmly where the bottom of the pan joins the sides. Then press the crust against the pan's sides, shaping it so that the edges are flush with the rim. Place the crust in the freezer for 15 minutes.

Remove the crust from the freezer and spread the Chocolate Mousse over the bottom. Arrange the sliced strawberries on top. Chill for at least 1 hour before serving. Serve chilled or at room temperature. Covered with plastic wrap in the refrigerator, Chocolate Tart with Strawberries will keep for three days.

## Variation

• **For Chocolate Mousse Tart with Raspberries:** Replace the sliced fresh strawberries with 2 cups fresh raspberries.

*Silky chocolate mousse and sweet, juicy strawberries . . . this tart is elegant enough for any occasion.*

## Equipment

measuring cups
measuring spoons
cutting board
paring knife
pie plate, or tart pan with removable bottom, 9-inch

# Mousses, Puddings, and Sweet Sauces

These are your most versatile dessert recipes, great to keep on hand for preparing a gourmet raw treat at the last minute. Sweet sauces can garnish many desserts. Try Vanilla Crème Sauce (page 166) on Apple Crisp (page 147), and Raspberry Sauce (page 165) on Flourless Chocolate Cake (page 138). Puddings and mousses can be eaten straight or used to fill pies and tarts. If you have Chocolate Mousse (page 160) on hand, Chocolate Tart with Strawberries (page 157) can be made in ten minutes. Or you can combine mousses, puddings, and sweet sauces with fresh fruit to create a parfait. Use a small wine glass to present the parfait. Layer one or two mousses, puddings, or sweet sauces with sliced fruits or berries of different colors, such as strawberries, kiwifruit, bananas, mangoes, pineapple, and blackberries. Continue to layer until the wine glass is full. Try Key Lime Mousse (page 159) with Mango Pudding (page 163) and fresh blackberries and banana slices, or Chocolate Mousse (page 160) with Vanilla Crème Sauce (page 166) and raspberries.

# Key Lime Mousse

Yield: 1 cup, 2 servings

You need only three ingredients to make this luscious, bright green mousse.

$^3/_4$ cup mashed avocados (1 $^1/_2$ avocados)

$^1/_4$ cup raw honey or agave nectar

2 tablespoons fresh lime juice

Sliced fresh kiwifruit and/or berries, for garnish (optional)

## Equipment

fork
measuring cups
measuring spoons
food processor
rubber spatula

Place the avocados, honey, and lime juice in a food processor fitted with the S blade and process until smooth. Stop occasionally to scrape down the sides of the bowl with a rubber spatula. Garnish with kiwifruit slices and/or berries, if desired. Serve immediately.

## Variations

• **For a Double-Batch Key Lime Mousse:** Increase the amounts to 1 $^1/_2$ cups mashed avocados (3 avocados), $^1/_2$ cup raw honey or agave nectar, and $^1/_4$ cup fresh lime juice. Yield: 2 cups, 4 servings.

• **For Lemon Mousse:** Replace the lime juice with an equal amount of fresh lemon juice.

• **For Key Lime Sherbet:** Freeze the Key Lime Mousse for at least 4 hours. Allow to thaw for 15 minutes before serving. Stored in a sealed container, Key Lime Sherbet will keep for up to one month in the freezer.

# Chocolate Mousse

See photo facing page 161

*No one will know that avocado replaces butter, cream, and eggs in this silky mousse.*

## Equipment

fork
measuring cups
measuring spoons
food processor
rubber spatula

Yield: 1 cup, 2 servings

$^1/_4$ cup pitted medjool dates, soaked
$^1/_4$ cup pure maple syrup or agave nectar
$^1/_2$ teaspoon vanilla extract (optional)
$^3/_4$ cup mashed avocados (1 $^1/_2$ avocados)
$^1/_4$ cup plus 2 tablespoons unsweetened cocoa or carob powder
$^1/_4$ cup water

Place the dates, maple syrup, and optional vanilla in a food processor fitted with the S blade and process until smooth. Add the avocado and cocoa powder and process until creamy. Stop occasionally to scrape down the sides of the bowl with a rubber spatula. Add the water and process briefly. Stored in a sealed container, Chocolate Mousse will keep for three days in the refrigerator or two weeks in the freezer. Serve chilled or at room temperature.

## Variations

• **For Double-Batch Chocolate Mousse:** Increase the amounts to $^1/_2$ cup pitted medjool dates, soaked, $^1/_2$ cup pure maple syrup, 1 teaspoon vanilla extract, 1 $^1/_2$ cups mashed avocados (3 avocados), $^3/_4$ cup cocoa or carob powder, and $^1/_2$ cup water. Yield: 2 cups, 4 servings.

*See more variations on page 161*

*Tropical Fruit Tart, page 156, with Mango Pudding, page 163, and Coconut Crust, page 145*

## Variations for Chocolate Mousse (continued)

• **For Chocolate Buttercream Frosting:** Omit the water.

• **For Chocolate Sauce:** Increase the water to $\frac{1}{2}$ cup for a small batch, and to 1 cup for a double batch.

• **For Chocolate Ice Cream:** Freeze the Chocolate Mousse for at least 4 hours. Allow to thaw for 15 minutes before serving. Stored in a sealed container, Chocolate Ice Cream will keep for one month in the freezer.

# Banana Pudding

Yield: 2 servings

$\frac{1}{2}$ cup Vanilla Crème Sauce (page 166)
1 banana, cut in half
$\frac{1}{4}$ cup Crumble Topping (page 144)

To make the creamy banana custard, place the Vanilla Crème Sauce and half of the banana in a blender and process until smooth. Thinly slice the other banana half. Place 2 tablespoons of the Crumble Topping in a small bowl. Layer half of the banana slices, $\frac{1}{4}$ cup of the banana custard, the rest of the banana slices, and the remaining banana custard. Top with the remaining 2 tablespoons of Crumble Topping. Serve immediately.

*Flourless Chocolate Cake, page 139, with Raspberry Sauce, page 165*

*parfait of Chocolate Mousse, page 160, and
Vanilla Crème Sauce, page 166*

*This is the old-fashioned kind of pudding, with mock graham cracker crumble, creamy custard, and banana slices.*

## Equipment
measuring cups
measuring spoons
cutting board
paring knife
blender
rubber spatula
small bowl

# Lemon Glaze

*The perfect frosting for Walnut-Raisin Cake (page 134).*

## Equipment

measuring cups
measuring spoons
food processor
rubber spatula

Yield: $1/2$ cup, 4 servings

$1/2$ cup pitted medjool dates, soaked
2 tablespoons fresh lemon juice
2 tablespoons water

Place the dates, lemon juice, and water in a food processor fitted with the S blade and process until smooth. Stop occasionally to scrape down the sides of the bowl with a rubber spatula. Stored in a sealed container in the refrigerator, Lemon Glaze will keep for five days.

## Variations

• **For Double-Batch Lemon Glaze:** Increase the amounts to 1 cup pitted dates, soaked, $1/4$ cup fresh lemon juice, and $1/4$ cup water. Yield: 1 cup, 8 servings.

• **For Orange Glaze:** Replace the lemon juice and water with $1/4$ cup fresh orange juice for a small batch, and $1/2$ cup for a double batch.

# Mango Pudding

Yield: 1 cup, 2 servings

1½ cups chopped fresh mangoes (2 mangoes) or
    frozen mango chunks, thawed and drained
½ cup chopped dried mangoes (cut into pieces
    with a scissors), soaked 10 minutes and drained
¼ cup sliced kiwifruit, blueberries, or
    blackberries (optional)

Place the fresh and dried mangoes in a blender and process on high speed until smooth. Transfer to a serving bowl and top with the kiwifruit, if desired. Stored in a sealed container in the refrigerator, Mango Pudding will keep for three days. Serve chilled or at room temperature.

## Variations:

• **For Double-Batch Mango Pudding:** Increase the amounts to 3 cups chopped fresh mangoes (4 mangoes) and 1 cup chopped dried mangoes, soaked. Yield: 2 cups, 4 servings.

• **For Pineapple Pudding:** Replace the fresh and dried mangoes with equal amounts of fresh and dried pineapple.

*See photo facing page 160*

*Don't let the simple ingredient list fool you—this fat-free pudding is rich and creamy.*

## Equipment

measuring cups
kitchen scissors
blender
rubber spatula

# Sweet Orange Cream Sauce

*Serve with Tropical Fruit Salad
(page 50) for an elegant
breakfast or brunch.*

## Equipment

citrus juicer or reamer
measuring cups
measuring spoons
blender
rubber spatula

Yield: 1 cup, 4 servings

1 cup soaked raw cashews
1/4 cup fresh orange juice
2 tablespoons raw honey or agave nectar
2 tablespoons water

Place all the ingredients in a blender and process on high speed until smooth. Chill for at least 30 minutes before serving. Stored in a sealed container in the refrigerator, Sweet Orange Cream Sauce will keep for three days.

## Variation

• For Sweet Lemon Cream Sauce: Replace the orange juice with 2 tablespoons fresh lemon juice and increase the water to 1/4 cup.

# Raspberry Sauce

Yield: 1 cup

1 cup fresh or frozen raspberries (thaw and drain,
   if frozen)
¼ cup pitted medjool dates, soaked

Place all the ingredients in a blender and process until smooth.
Stored in a sealed container in the refrigerator, Raspberry Sauce
will keep for three days.

## Variation

- **For other fruit sauces:** Replace the raspberries with an
  equal amount of fresh or frozen blackberries, blueberries,
  cherries, pineapple, or strawberries (thaw and drain, if
  frozen).

*This sauce is a classic
accompaniment to Flourless
Chocolate Cake (page 138).*

## Equipment

measuring cups
blender
rubber spatula

# Vanilla Crème Sauce

See photo facing page 161

*Serve this delicious sauce instead of whipped cream with fresh berries or with cakes, crisps, pies, and tarts.*

## Equipment

measuring cups
measuring spoons
blender
rubber spatula

Yield: 1 cup, 8 servings

1 cup soaked raw cashews
1/4 cup plus 2 tablespoons water
2 tablespoons pure maple syrup or agave nectar
1 teaspoon vanilla extract, or seeds of 1 vanilla
   bean

Place all the ingredients in a blender and process on high speed until smooth. Chill for at least 30 minutes before serving. Stored in a sealed container in the refrigerator, Vanilla Crème Sauce will keep for five days.

# Shakes and Ice Creams

If you love milkshakes and ice cream, try my Banana Shake (page 168) or a sorbet. Unlike heavy dairy-based shakes and ice creams, these frozen treats will leave you energized.

# Mango Sorbet

Yield: 1 serving

**1 cup frozen mango chunks (about 1 1/2 mangoes)**

Allow the frozen mango chunks to thaw for 5 minutes. Place in a food processor fitted with the S blade and process until smooth. Stop occasionally to scrape down the sides of the bowl with a rubber spatula. Serve immediately.

## Variation

• **For Cherry Sorbet:** Replace the mangoes with an equal amount of frozen pitted cherries. Place the cherries in a food processor fitted with the S blade and process until smooth.

## Equipment

measuring cups
food processor
rubber spatula

# Banana Shake

*Satisfies that milkshake craving.*

## Equipment

measuring cups
measuring spoons
blender
rubber spatula

Yield: I serving

1 frozen banana (page 30)
$\frac{1}{2}$ cup Almond Milk (page 28)
1 $\frac{1}{2}$ teaspoons pure maple syrup or agave nectar
$\frac{1}{2}$ teaspoon vanilla extract

Allow the banana to thaw for 5 minutes. Break the banana into two or three pieces and place it in a blender with the remaining ingredients. Process until smooth and creamy. Serve immediately.

## Variations

• **For Chocolate Shake:** Add 2 tablespoons unsweetened cocoa or carob powder, and increase the maple syrup to 2 teaspoons.

• **For Strawberry Shake:** Omit the vanilla extract and add I cup fresh or frozen strawberries (about 6). If using frozen strawberries, do not thaw or drain.

# Vanilla Ice Cream

Yield: 1 1/2 cups, 2 servings

1 1/2 cups Almond Cream (page 29)
2 tablespoons pure maple syrup or agave nectar
1/2 teaspoon vanilla extract, or seeds of 1 vanilla bean

Place all the ingredients in a mixing bowl and whisk to combine. Freeze in an ice cream maker according to the manufacturer's directions. Serve immediately.

*This easy ice cream tastes so rich and creamy, you won't believe it's dairy-free. It makes purchasing an ice cream maker worth it!*

## Equipment

measuring cups
measuring spoons
medium mixing bowl
whisk
ice cream maker

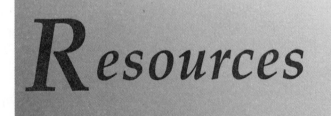

# Glossary and Resources

# Glossary

### agave nectar

A natural sweetener made from the juice of the agave plant. Agave nectar is 90 percent fructose and has a much lower glycemic index than honey, maple syrup, or cane sugar. Choose light agave nectar for mild sweetness, and dark agave for a deep, molasses-like flavor. Both light and dark agave are available through Nature's First Law (see Resources, page 187).

### aloe vera juice

The juice from the leaves of the aloe vera plant has been used for centuries for its soothing and healing properties. Look for whole leaf, preservative-free juice. I recommend Lily of the Desert Whole Leaf Aloe Vera Juice.

### almond butter

A spread made from ground raw almonds. Can be used to replace peanut butter, which is made from roasted nuts.

### apple cider vinegar, raw

A fruity vinegar made from apple juice. I recommend raw, unpasteurized vinegar, which contains beneficial bacteria and enzymes.

### antioxidants

Nutrients found in fruits and vegetables, including vitamins A and C, which help neutralize destructive free-radical molecules. Free radicals can contribute to cancer, diabetes, and other diseases.

### arugula

A salad green with a peppery, slightly bitter flavor. Also known as "rocket."

### automatic sprouter

An appliance that grows green leafy sprouts and wheatgrass. No daily rinsing or draining is required. I recommend the Tribest Fresh Life Automatic Sprouter.

### balsamic vinegar

An Italian vinegar made from grape juice, with a deep sweet-and-sour flavor. True balsamic vinegar (Aceto Balsamic Tradizionale) is aged for a minimum of 10 years in wooden casks. The finest and most expensive vinegars are aged for 25 to 50 years.

### bamboo sushi mat

A woven mat essential for making tight, professional nori rolls.

### beta-carotene

A nutrient found in green, red, and orange vegetables that the body converts into vitamin A.

### Black Mission figs

Purple-black figs with a deep, complex flavor.

### blender

An electric appliance that purées and liquefies. I recommend the two-speed Oster Classic Beehive model with glass container, the Kitchenaid KSB560 blender, and the Tribest Personal Blender for travel and/or single-serving smoothies. You may also wish to invest in a powerful high-speed blender, such as the Vita-Mix or K-Tec.

## blue-green algae

An excellent source of protein, chlorophyll, beta-carotene, and trace minerals. The three main types are Klamath Lake algae, spirulina, and chlorella. I recommend E-3 Live Klamath Lake Algae.

## Bragg Liquid Aminos

A seasoning made from soybeans and distilled water. Less salty than shoyu or tamari.

## Brazil nuts

These rich, creamy nuts are a concentrated source of the mineral selenium.

## Calimyrna figs

Golden-colored figs with honeylike flavor.

## capers

Pickled flower buds used in sauces and condiments.

## carob powder

A dark brown powder made from ground carob seeds and pods. Carob powder tastes similar to cocoa powder, but it has no caffeine and is naturally sweet. It may be purchased raw or roasted.

## chef's knife

A 7–10-inch knife with a broad blade and very sharp edge, designed for slicing, chopping, dicing, and mincing. I recommend an 8-inch knife for most tasks. You can purchase a European-style or a santoku Asian-style knife, depending on personal preference. My favorite brands are Henckels, Wüsthof, Mac, Global, Cutco, and the Kershaw Shun line. Kyocera ceramic knives are ideal for cutting fruit and lettuce, since they will not alter the delicate taste or color of these foods.

## citrus juicer/reamer

A wide cone with ridges that crushes the inside of halved citrus fruit, releasing the juice. Some models come with a dish to catch the juice; others are handheld. I recommend reamers that use interchangeable cones to accommodate the different sizes of limes, oranges, and grapefruits, such as the Oxo Good Grips Citrus Juicer. Electric juicers are efficient when you want to make larger quantities.

## cocoa powder, unsweetened

Unsweetened cocoa powder is made from raw or roasted cacao beans that have been processed to extract the cacao butter, then dried and ground. Use a naturally processed, organic brand, such as Rapunzel or Green and Black's. Raw cocoa powder is available through Nature's First Law (see Resources, page 187).

## coconut oil

A health-promoting, naturally saturated fat made up of medium-chain fatty acids, which are thought to increase metabolism and promote weight loss. I recommend Natural Zing's Organic Raw Virgin Coconut Oil.

## cremini mushroom

A small mushroom that is more flavorful than the common white button variety.

## cutting board

A surface for cutting fruits and vegetables, preferably made from wood or bamboo. I recommend John Boos and Totally Bamboo boards.

## dehydrator

An appliance for drying food indoors, used to make dried fruits and vegetables, seasoned nuts and seeds, fruit leathers, and raw breads, crackers, cookies, and bars. I recommend the Excalibur five- or nine-tray model, with Teflex sheets (which are essential if you will be drying wet mixtures, such as fruit leather and cracker batters).

## dice

To cut food into very small cubes, about ¼-inch.

## distilled water

Water that has been purified by boiling and condensation. The distilling process removes bacteria, viruses, heavy metals, and other pollutants, but also removes healthful mineral salts. Most of the newer water distillers also have a carbon filter in the unit, which removes chemicals such as chlorine and pesticides. I recommend the Tribest Purewise distiller.

## dulse flakes

A reddish-purple sea vegetable, ground into flakes and used as a salty condiment. Dulse flakes are high in iron and trace minerals.

## dried shiitake mushrooms

Mushrooms with an intense, earthy flavor. Soak in water for about 30 minutes to reconstitute.

## enzymes

Often called "the spark of life," enzymes are protein catalysts that produce energy to fuel our cells and bodily systems. Many of the enzymes in raw food can be absorbed and used by our cells to replenish our own stock of these catalysts.

## essential fatty acids (EFAs)

Important nutrients for growth, energy, mental state, and healthy skin and hair. The body cannot produce them and must obtain them through food. Rich sources include fish oils and seed oils, such as flaxseed and pumpkin seed. Refined oils, heated oils, hydrogenated oils, and saturated fats lack EFAs.

## Evert Fresh Green Bags

These produce bags absorb the gases that cause vegetables to deteriorate. Produce stored in these bags instead of plastic bags will keep at least three times longer.

## extra-virgin olive oil

A delicious, fruity oil resulting from the first pressing of tree-ripened olives using a low temperature and chemical-free process that involves only mechanical pressure. Extra-virgin olive oil is rich in healthy monounsaturated fats.

## file grater

A grater with tiny, razor-like edges, ideal for removing the zest from citrus fruits and for grating ginger, nutmeg, parmesan cheese, and chocolate. I recommend the Microplane brand.

## filtered water

Water that has been filtered through a carbon block to remove chlorine and other chemicals as well as heavy metals, such as lead and mercury. I recommend Aquasana filters for the countertop or below the sink.

## flaxseeds

Tiny seeds, available brown or golden, which are an excellent source of omega-3 fatty acids and fiber. To preserve the delicate oils, flaxseeds should be consumed raw. Grind them in a coffee grinder immediately before eating.

## flaxseed oil

A nutritious oil rich in omega-3 fatty acids. As a supplement, take one or two tablespoons a day, on salads or in a smoothie. Flaxseed oil is very fragile and should never be heated. I recommend Barleans and Omega Nutrition brands.

## food processor

A machine with interchangeable blades and cutting disks and a removable bowl and lid. Used for chopping, grinding, puréeing, slicing, and shredding ingredients. I recommend the Cuisinart Pro Plus (3-cup capacity) for smaller tasks, and the Cuisinart 7, 11, and 14-cup capacity models for larger tasks. A 7-cup machine is fine for regular home use, but if you plan to prepare food for large numbers of people, a 14-cup machine is essential. At under $100, the Hamilton Beach 14-cup food processor is an excellent value.

## frisée

This salad green has a mildly bitter flavor and feathery texture. It is often used in mesclun mixes. If unavailable, substitute curly endive.

## glycemic index

A measuring system that ranks foods according to how much they raise blood sugar levels.

## goji berries

Goji berries are one of the most nutritionally dense fruits available. They are a rich source of complete protein, vitamin C, and trace minerals. Goji berries are delicious whether eaten straight or soaked before adding to fruit smoothies.

## green powders

Nutritious whole-food supplements made from dehydrated wheat, kamut, and barley grasses, blue-green algae, and/or dehydrated green leafy vegetables. There are many good brands available—some that I have used include Perfect Food (Garden of Life), Green Kamut, Vitamineral Green, and Pure Synergy.

## hemp seeds

These tiny, mild-flavored seeds are a concentrated source of complete protein and omega-3 fatty acids. I recommend grinding them in a coffee grinder and adding them to juices and smoothies.

## honing steel

A long rod that realigns the edges of your knives to keep them sharp. To hone, draw your knife at a 20-degree angle, from base to tip, along the steel. Repeat several times on each side of the blade. Use your steel every time you use your knife and you won't have to sharpen it for months.

## hydrogenated oils

Unhealthful vegetable oils that have been hardened by heating at very high temperatures while injecting hydrogen gas. This process destroys the essential fatty acids in the oil and replaces them with harmful trans-fatty acids.

## ice cream maker

A machine that produces ice cream by rotating a canister around a paddle. The canister, which holds a freezing agent, must be placed in the freezer for at least several hours before using. I recommend the Cuisinart brand, which costs about $60.

## juicer

An electrical appliance that extracts the juice of fruits and vegetables. A slow-speed, low-temperature model is best, since it produces the maximum yield and preserves more nutrients and enzymes. I recommend Tribest juicers (Solostar or Green Star models) and the Omega 8003.

## julienne

To cut into matchstick strips.

## kale

A cruciferous vegetable with dark green, wrinkled leaves. Varieties include curly green kale, red kale, and dinosaur kale (also called lacinato kale). I prefer the dinosaur variety, since its flatter leaves are easier to cut into thin strips for salads and to feed into the juicer for green drinks.

## kitchen scissors

High-quality kitchen shears are perfect for cutting broccoli florets, snipping kale into thin strips, and opening plastic packaging.

## knife block

A wooden block with slats designed for knife storage. The block sits on your countertop, so your knives are readily available, organized, and protected. You can also purchase an in-drawer knife holder to save countertop space.

## knife sharpener

There are two types of knife sharpeners: natural stone and commercial. To use a sharpening stone, first read the instructions to determine if your stone needs to be soaked in water or mineral oil. Then draw the knife toward you across the stone at a 20-degree angle several times, from base to tip. Repeat on the other side of the blade. To use a commercial knife sharpener (I recommend Chef's Choice manual sharpener or a sharpener that is designed for your particular brand of knives), refer to the instruction booklet that comes with it. Serrated, ceramic, and very fine knives should be sharpened professionally.

## mandoline

A utensil with a variety of blades for slicing and julienning fruits and vegetables uniformly. Traditional steel mandolines cost over $100, but the inexpensive Japanese versions (under $25) do fine. I also recommend the Oxo Good Grips Mandoline and the Borner V-Slicer. Another option is the ceramic slicer, made by Kyocera. It is similar to a mandoline, but its blade stays sharp longer than steel and will not alter the taste or color of foods. It does not have multiple blades for different thicknesses, but it is ideal for paper-thin slices of cucumber or onion.

## maple sugar

Maple sugar is created when the sap of the sugar maple is boiled for longer than is needed to create maple syrup. It may be used to replace whole cane sugar in many recipes, if desired.

## marinate

To flavor and tenderize ingredients by letting them stand in a dressing of oil, acid (such as citrus juice), and salt.

## mason jars

These glass jars are useful for storing staple ingredients, salad dressings, and sauces, for soaking nuts and seeds, for shaking green powders and ground flaxseeds into juice, for transporting drinks and soups to work, and for growing sprouts. I recommend pint- and quart-size jars with wide-mouth openings and metal screw-top lids.

## medjool dates

"Nature's candy," this intensely sweet and sticky fruit has amber-colored, wrinkled skin and a chewy texture. Always buy soft dates, for easiest processing in raw food recipes. Pit the dates yourself; they are fresher than pre-pitted. Medjool dates are the largest and sweetest soft dates. I also recommend Honey, Halawi, and Black Sphinx varieties. Stored in an airtight container in the refrigerator, medjool dates will keep for six months.

## mesclun greens

Mixed young salad greens, which often include baby romaine, red leaf, and oak leaf lettuces, arugula, frisée, mâche, and radicchio. Choose greens with crisp leaves and no signs of wilting. Refrigerate in a plastic bag for up to five days, and wash and spin dry just before using.

## mince

To chop very fine. Ingredients most commonly minced are onions, celery, garlic, ginger, and fresh herbs.

## miso

A paste made from fermented soybeans and salt. Miso is rich in enzymes and healthy bacteria. Buy unpasteurized miso, available in the refrigerated section of most natural food stores. I recommend mellow white miso, which is sweet and mild and lends a rich flavor to soups and sauces.

## nori seaweed

Thin, dried seaweed sheets used to wrap sushi. You can purchase nori either raw or toasted.

## parfait

A layered dessert made from ice cream or mousse, fruit, and a dessert sauce or whipped cream. Parfaits are traditionally served in tall, narrow dessert or wine glasses.

## pâté

A finely ground spread or filling, well-seasoned with onions or garlic, salt, and herbs. Raw pâtés are made from nuts, seeds, and vegetables.

## phytonutrients

Natural compounds found in plant foods, thought to enhance the immune system, slow the aging process, and help prevent heart disease and cancer. Common phytonutrients include bioflavanoids, carotenoids, lycopene, and chlorophyll.

## portobello mushrooms

Large cremini mushrooms with a meaty texture. Stuff with any pâté or dip for an instant entrée.

## protein powder

A refined supplement used to boost the protein content of one's diet. Protein powders may be made from whey, milk, egg, soy, brown rice, or hemp. I recommend Goatein Pure Goat's Milk Protein (Garden of Life), Raw Organic Hemp Protein Powder (Nutiva), and Thor's Raw Power! Protein Superfood Blend (Nature's First Law).

## pumpkin seed oil

A nutty tasting cold-pressed oil, delicious on salads. Pumpkin seed oil is a rich source of essential fatty acids and is thought to balance hormones. I recommend the Omega Nutrition brand.

## radicchio

A peppery, bitter, crunchy salad green with red and white leaves and a tight head.

## ramekin

A small ceramic dish, about three inches in diameter and six ounces in volume. Ramekins are ideal for individual servings of crisps, mousses, and puddings.

## raw food

Food that is unprocessed, unrefined, and untreated with heat.

## raw honey

Pure, natural honey that has not been processed by heating. Raw honey is rich in enzymes.

## raw olives

Olives naturally cured and sun-dried at low temperatures, without chemicals.

## raw milk cheese

Cheese made from unpasteurized cow, goat, or sheep milk. These cheeses are rich in minerals and enzymes and are easier to digest than pasteurized types.

## rice paper

A round spring roll wrapper made from rice flour and water. Available in dried form, it must be softened in water before using.

## romaine heart

Romaine lettuce heads that have been trimmed down to the succulent inner leaves. They typically come in packs of three.

## salad spinner

A tool that washes and spin-dries salad greens so they are as dry as possible before dressing is added.

## salt, unrefined

Sun-dried salt, with its natural mineral content intact. I recommend Celtic Sea Salt and Himalayan Crystal Salt.

## saturated fat

A type of fat that is solid at room temperature. It is found in the highest concentrations in high-fat dairy products, red meats, coconut oil, cocoa butter, palm kernel oil, and palm oil. Saturated fats are more heat-stable than other oils, so if you do sauté your foods, I recommend using coconut oil. Olive oil has some saturated fat in addition to monounsaturated fat, and is stable for sautéing at lower temperatures.

## serrated knife, 5-inch

A small, razor-sharp, maneuverable knife ideal for cutting tomatoes, removing the peel from citrus fruits, and slicing soft fruits such as peaches, plums, and kiwifruit.

## shallots

Tiny, delicately flavored onions, often used in French cooking, especially salad dressings and sauces.

## shoyu

A salty seasoning made from fermented soybeans and wheat. Commonly called soy sauce.

## spatula

A versatile utensil available in a variety of shapes and sizes, made from metal or rubber. Spatulas with sturdy, flexible, rubber heads are best for mixing and removing mixtures from the food processor. Purchase one with a skinnier head as well, for removing mixtures from the bottom of the blender. Flexible, narrow, metal spatulas are ideal for frosting cakes, and metal spatulas with wide, offset heads are essential for lifting slices of cake or pie from the pan. Purchase a square one for serving lasagne, brownies, and square-shaped pieces of cake, and a triangular one for serving pies and tarts.

## spring water

Mineral-rich water pumped from natural springs in the earth. There are many excellent brands; I enjoy the taste of Trinity and Voss.

## sprouts

Nuts, seeds, grains, or legumes that have been soaked, drained, and left to germinate. Sprouts are rich in vitamins, minerals, phytonutrients, protein, and amino acids.

## sprout bag

A mesh bag used to grow sprouts or to strain nut and seed milks.

## stevia

A naturally sweet South American herb that contains no calories or carbohydrates and will not raise blood sugar levels.

## sun-dried tomatoes

Plum tomatoes that have been dried at low temperatures to a chewy texture and tart-sweet taste. They are available oil-packed or dry. Dry tomatoes must be soaked for 30 minutes before using. I recommend the Sonoma brand.

## S blade

The blade of a food processor that is used for chopping, grinding, and puréeing.

## tahini

A creamy paste made from raw, hulled sesame seeds. Sesame butter is ground from whole (unhulled) sesame seeds, and is heavier in taste and texture.

## tamari

A traditional Japanese soy sauce made without wheat. Tamari has a rich, salty, wine-like flavor.

## tart pan

A straight-sided pan with fluted edges, used for making pastries. These pans come in a variety of shapes and sizes; they may be round or rectangular and range from 4 to 12 inches across. Look for a pan with a removable bottom, which allows you to release the outer ring while leaving the crust intact.

## trans-fats

Trans-fatty acids are created when vegetable oils are hydrogenated, refined or heated at high temperatures, or go rancid due to overexposure to air and light. Many snack foods, crackers, breads, and cookies contain these unnatural fats. Trans-fats compete with essential fatty acids for absorption, creating metabolic imbalances and deposits in the arteries.

## unhulled sesame seeds

Brown sesame seeds with the hull intact. Unhulled sesame seeds have more calcium than hulled, white seeds

## vegetable spiral slicer

Also called "the garnishing machine," this gadget transforms zucchini and other vegetables into delicate angel hair pasta.

## Vita-Mix

A high-speed, high-performance blender that makes smoothies, sauces, soups, and nut milks in seconds. Purchase the 5200 model, which gives you greater control over speeds.

## watercress

A crisp, leafy salad green with a slightly bitter, peppery flavor. Sold in small bunches.

## whole cane sugar

Naturally squeezed, dried, and ground sugarcane juice. I recommend Rapadura whole cane sugar. If unavailable, substitute organic Sucanat, or maple sugar.

## whole oat groats

A tender grain with a mild sweetness. Whole groats are oats before they have been flattened into familiar rolled oats. Look for groats that are untreated with heat, since sometimes manufacturers steam them to increase shelf life.

## zest

The outermost skin layer of citrus fruit, removed with a zester, peeler, or file grater. Remove only the colored portion of the skin, not the bitter white pith beneath.

# Resources

*There are many excellent raw food books and Web sites. Here are some that I have had personal experience with.*

## Books and Videos

**Raw Food Made Easy DVD**
Jennifer Cornbleet
**www.learnrawfood.com**
A great companion item to the book, this informative and entertaining DVD expands on the recipes and tips found in *Raw Food Made Easy for 1 or 2 People.*

**Angel Foods: Healthy Recipes for Heavenly Bodies**
Cherie Soria
**www.rawfoodchef.com**
Over 240 delicious and easy-to-prepare cooked and raw vegan recipes. Includes an excellent chapter on sprouting and kitchen gardening.

**Conscious Eating**
Gabriel Cousens, MD
**www.amazon.com**
This comprehensive reference guide to raw food nutrition draws on the perspectives of metabolic typing and Ayurvedic medicine.

**Eating in the Raw: A Beginner's Guide to Getting Slimmer, Feeling Healthier, and Looking Younger the Raw-Food Way**
Carol Alt
**www.amazon.com**
Presents practical information on how to adapt to a high raw diet without deprivation. Carol's flexible approach includes how to eat raw if you aren't vegetarian, how to eat raw at restaurants, and how to incorporate some cooked food into your diet.

**Elaina's Pure Joy Kitchen Recipe Binder**
Elaina Love
**www.purejoyplanet.com**
Over 100 easy-to-use, delicious recipes for the whole family. Recipes are covered with page protectors and arranged in a three-ring binder. Videos include *Introduction to Living Foods, Journey to Natural Beauty*, and *Holiday Feast*.

**Henckels Knife Skill Instructional Video**
**www.amazon.com**
This video teaches you how to slice, chop, dice, and mince like a professional chef.

**Living Cuisine: The Art and Spirit of Raw Foods**
Renée Loux Underkoffler
**www.amazon.com**
A comprehensive resource for raw nutrition, ingredients, equipment, and techniques, plus over 300 delicious and varied recipes.

**Living on Live Food, book and DVD**
Alissa Cohen
**www.alissacohen.com**
Chapter topics include: shopping for raw and living foods, how to start raw today, four-week shopping and preparation guide, and recipes. The 3.5 hour DVD offers clear instructions for easy recipes and techniques, and answers frequently asked raw food questions.

**The Raw Food Detox Diet: The Five-Step Plan for Vibrant Health and Maximum Weight Loss**
Natalia Rose
**www.therawfooddetoxdiet.com**
Natalia provides five levels of menu plans and recipes to detoxify the body and transition to a raw food diet. She explains how you can achieve the bene-fits of eating raw whatever your present diet or state of health. This book contains an excellent chapter on food combining for easy digestion and weight loss.

**The Raw Gourmet**
Nomi Shannon
**www.rawgourmet.com**
A beautiful book with full-color photographs, filled with simple and elegant recipes for all occasions. Includes a sample menu plan for a three-week cleanse diet.

**Whole Foods Companion: A Guide for Adventurous Cooks, Curious Shoppers, and Lovers of Natural Foods**
Dianne Onstad
**www.amazon.com**
An encyclopedic guide to hundreds of natural foods, including fruits, vegetables, nuts, seeds, oils, grains, legumes, herbs, and spices. Includes nutritional information, lore, and legends.

## Learn Raw Food

Jennifer Cornbleet, director
My Web site **www.learnrawfood.com** is the complete online companion to this book. It gives you access to tools including recipes, and a free monthly newsletter. It's also the place to go to find out about upcoming classes and workshops. Private individual and group classes are also available.

## The Conscious Health Institute

**www.ConsciousHealthInstitute.org**
A holistic not-for-profit institute whose mission is to teach people how to become active participants in their own life-health, and how to stay healthy through self-responsible living. Offers a bi-monthly online newsletter.

## Karyn's Inner Beauty Center

Karyn Calabrese, owner and director
**www.karynraw.com**
Offers a four-week detoxification program in Chicago, meeting in weekly two-hour sessions, that helps people lose weight and restore and rejuvenate their bodies. The program takes you step-by-step through a cleanse, using the tools of raw food nutrition, supplementation, juice fasting, and other holistic therapies.

## Living and Raw Foods

**www.living-foods.com**
The largest community on the Internet, dedicated to educating the world about the power of living and raw foods.

## Living Light Culinary Arts Institute

Cherie Soria and Dan Ladermann, codirectors
**www.rawfoodchef.com**
Certification courses in raw culinary arts for individuals, chefs, and teachers. LLCAI can help you find services in your area through their chef and teacher placement service. Located in Fort Bragg, California.

## Pure Joy Planet

Elaina Love
**www.purejoyplanet.com**
Hands-on coaching, phone consultations, classes, and workshops.

## Holistic Health Practitioner

**Keyvan Golestaneh, MA, LAc**
lapis-holistic@comcast.net
415-462-6167
**www.lapisholistichealth.com**
Keyvan Golestaneh is a healer and yoga
teacher who has studied Asian yogic
traditions and meditation for over 25
years. Working within a naturopathic
tradition, he incorporates bioenergetic
healing, herbal therapy, and Chinese,
Ayurvedic, and Isopathic medicines. He
emphasizes taking responsibility for
one's health and life through self-
development, dietary/nutritional
education, and exercise. Keyvan has a
master's degree in counseling
psychology and is certified in Chinese
Medicine, Structural Body Therapy, and
Jin Shin Do. He also has extensive
training in body-centered psychotherapy.
Based in San Diego, California, he
conducts workshops internationally and
offers consultations and therapy
worldwide during his travels and by
appointment via phone. Keyvan can
work with any health problems you may
have. Whenever necessary, he helps find
local sources for appropriate health and
healing modalities.

## Supplements

**Garden of Life**
**www.gardenoflife.com**
Goatein Pure Goat's Milk Protein Powder.

**Nutiva**
**www.nutiva.com**
Raw Organic Hemp Protein Powder.

**Ralph Plantwagon**
**www.ralphplantwagon.com**
Nutritional supplements with superior
bioavailability, made from 100 percent
food concentrates (WholeState™).
Multivitamin-mineral, calcium-
magnesium, vitamin C, digestive
enzymes, and joint-tissue formulas are
available.

**The Synergy Company**
**www.synergy-co.com**
Pure Synergy Green Superfood.

**Vision E3 Live**
**www.e3live.com**
Fresh-frozen Klamath Lake algae.

# Kitchen Equipment

**Ace Hardware**
www.acehardware.com
Ball mason jars.

**Aquasana**
www.aquasana.com
Water filters.

**Cuisinart**
www.cuisinart.com
High-quality food processors.

**Cutco**
www.cutco.com
Knives. I recommend the kitchen shears, petite chef's knife, vegetable knife, cleaver, trimmer knife, 2 ¾-inch paring knife, and peeler.

**Discount Juicers**
www.discountjuicers.com
Juicers and other raw food appliances.

**Evert Fresh Green Bags**
www.greenbags.com
Produce storage bags.

**Mac Knives**
www.macknife.com
Fine, razor-sharp knives.

**Living Light Marketplace**
www.rawfoodchef.com
Online shopping for products for healthy living and the raw food kitchen: culinary supplies, juicers, dehydrators, spiral slicers, mandolines, quality blenders, woodenware, cutlery, kitchen gadgets of all kinds, culinary videos, books, organic vegan body products, and specialty foods.

**Pure Joy Planet**
www.purejoyplanet.com
Vegetable spiral slicers and sprout bags.

**Sur La Table**
www.surlatable.com
A comprehensive selection of the best kitchen equipment and utensils.

**Target**
www.target.com
Oster Classic blenders and affordable kitchen equipment.

**Tribest**
www.tribest.com
Tribest manufactures some of the best raw food kitchen appliances, including the Green Star and Solostar juicers and the Personal Blender, a small, lightweight blender ideal for travel.

**Bragg**
www.bragg.com
Liquid Aminos seasoning and raw apple cider vinegar.

**Diamond Organics**
www.diamondorganics.com
Overnight delivery of organic groceries and produce.

**Frey Vineyards**
www.freywine.com
Organic, biodynamic wines, with no added sulfites.

**Good Stuff by Mom and Me**
www.gimmegoodstuff.com
Snacks, handmade fresh daily, from the highest-quality raw, vegan, organic, gluten-free, and germinated ingredients. The Pecan Pie Bars are my favorite!

**Gold Mine Natural Food Co.**
www.goldminenaturalfood.com
Nuts and seeds, dried fruits, sea vegetables, miso, and organic shoyu and tamari.

**The Grain and Salt Society**
www.celtic-seasalt.com
High-quality, unrefined sea salt.

**Himalayan Crystal Salt**
www.himalayancrystalsalt.com
Hand-mined, hand-packed salt, rich in all the natural minerals found in the human body.

**High Vibe Health and Healing**
www.highvibe.com
High Vibe, flourishing since 1993, has raw snacks, raw food staples, whole food vitamins and supplements, organic dried fruits, appliances, the finest beauty products, and a large selection of health-related books. Wholesale and retail are available. High Vibe ships worldwide.

**Joseph Mercola, DO**
www.mercola.com
Raw milk cheeses.

**Mail Order Catalog for Healthy Eating**
www.healthy-eating.com
Organic sprouting seeds, sprouting equipment, books, Evert Fresh bags, and spiralizers.

**Matter of Flax**
www.matterofflax.com
Healthy and delicious crackers made from flaxseeds, vegetables, and seasonings.

**Nature's First Law**
www.rawfood.com
Hundreds of high-quality raw foods and products at low prices, including raw, organic olives, agave nectar, raw cashews, raw carob and cocoa powder, and goji berries.

**Natural Zing**
www.naturalzing.com
Raw, organic food and health products.

**Omega Nutrition**
www.omeganutrition.com
Fresh, organic, unrefined oils.

**One Lucky Duck**
www.oneluckyduck.com
Delicious prepared raw foods, including
macaroons, biscotti, crackers, granola,
and ice cream.

**Organic Pastures**
www.organicpastures.com
Raw dairy products.

**Rapunzel Pure Organics**
www.rapunzel.com
Rapadura whole cane sugar and organic
cocoa powder.

**The Raw Bakery**
www.rawbakery.com
Breads, crackers, candies, brownies,
cakes, cookies, breakfast cereals, and
more, shipped to your door. The Raw
Bakery sells truly raw rolled oats and
muesli, as well as a grain mill for making
your own from whole oat groats.

**Really Raw Honey**
www.reallyrawhoney.com
Delicious, unrefined, unheated honey.

**Rejuvenative Foods**
www.rejuvenativefoods.com
Raw organic nut and seed butters

**Sun Organic Farms**
www.sunorganic.com
High-quality nuts and seeds, dried fruits,
dates, oils, nut butters, and carob
powder.

**Sprout People**
www.sproutpeople.com
Tasty green leafy sprout mixes and whole
oat groats.

**Trader Joe's**
www.traderjoes.com
Unique, high-quality groceries at
affordable prices.

**Trinity**
www.trinitysprings.com
Exceptional-tasting, mineral-rich spring
water.

**Voss Water**
www.vosswater.com
Pure artesian water from Norway, in
attractive glass bottles.

**Whole Foods Market**
www.wholefoodsmarket.com
This nationwide chain offers a wide
variety of organic produce.

# Index

*Page numbers in italics indicate recipes using the cited recipe.*

bananas
  Almond Sunflower Cereal, 51
  Berry Smoothie, 47
  Frozen, 30
  Granola, 52
  Piña Colada Smoothie, 48
  Pudding, 161
  Shake, 168
  Strawberry Shake, 168
  Tropical Fruit Salad, 50
  Yogurt Smoothie, 47
basil
  Caprese Salad, 97
  Olive Tapenade, 67
  Pesto, 70
  Pesto Dressing, 101
beets
  Fasting Juice, 42
  -Carrot-Celery Juice, 39
  peeling, 95
  Pink Apple Juice, 39
  Salad, Shaved, 95
  Sweet Energizing-Purifying Juice, 41
berries. *See also* specific berries
  and Almond Cream, 49
  Almond Sunflower Cereal, 51
  Granola, 52
  Key Lime Mousse, 159
  and Orange Smoothie, 47
  Smoothie, 47
  Yogurt Smoothie, 47
beta-carotene, 172
beverages. *See also* juices and juicing; smoothies
  Almond Milk(s), 28
  Lemon Water, 44
  Sesame Milk, 29
blackberries
  Berries and Almond Cream, 49
  Berry Smoothie, 47
  Crisp, 148–149
  Mango Pudding, 163
  Spanish Fig Cake, 136
  Tropical Fruit Tart, 156
Black Forest Cake, 139
blenders, 24, 172
blueberries
  Berries and Almond Cream, 49
  Berry Smoothie, 47
  Crisp, 149

  Key Lime Tart, 150–151
  Mango Pudding, 163
  Muesli, 53
  Pie or Tart, 154–155
  Spanish Fig Cake, 136
  Tropical Fruit Tart, 156
blue cheese
  Harvest Salad with Cheese, 92
  Shaved Beet Salad with Cheese, 95
blue-green algae, 173
  Complete Meal Energizing-Purifying
    Juice, 41
  Complete Meal Green Juice, 43
bok choy
  Asian Greens, 131
Bragg Liquid Aminos, 173
Brazil nuts, 173
  Brazil Nut Milk, 29
broccoli
  Antioxidant Juice, 43
  Crudités, 87
  Energizing-Purifying Juice, 40
  Fasting Juice, 42
  Marinated Vegetables, 129
Brownies, 142

# C

cabbage
  Antioxidant Juice, 43
  Coleslaw, 126
  Energizing-Purifying Juice, 40
  Fasting Juice, 42
  Latin American, 127
  Pressed, 31, *126*
  Spring Rolls, 117
Caesar Salad, 86
cakes
  Apple Crumb, 135
  Black Forest, 139
  Chocolate:
    Buttercream Frosting, 139
    Flourless, 138
    Layer, with Raspberry Filling, 138
    with Raspberry Sauce, 139
  Spanish Fig, 136
  Walnut-Raisin, 134
California Not Tuna Rolls, 113
California Rolls, 112–113
cane sugar, whole, 180

# BOOK PUBLISHING COMPANY

*since 1974—books that educate, inspire, and empower*

**To find your favorite vegetarian and soyfood products online, visit:**
**www.healthy-eating.com**

*Other great titles by*
*Jennifer Cornbleet*

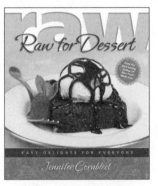

***Raw for Dessert***
Jennifer Cornbleet
*978-1-57067-236-1*
*$14.95*

***Raw Food Made Easy***
*DVD*
Jennifer Cornbleet
*978-1-57067-203-3   $19.95*

***Becoming Raw***
Brenda Davis, RD &
Vesanto Melina, MS, RD
978-1-57067-238-5
$24.95

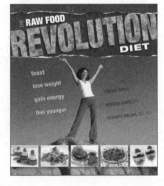

***The Raw Food Revolution***
***Diet***
Cherie Soria, Brenda Davis, RD
& Vesanto Melina, MS, RD
*978-1-57067-185-2*
*$21.95*

***Alive in 5***
Angela Elliott
*978-1-57067-202-6*
*$14.95*

***Raw Food Celebrations***
Nomi Shannon
Sheryl Duruz
*978-1-57067-228-6*
*$19.95*

**Purchase these health titles and cookbooks from your local bookstore or**
**natural food store, or you can buy them directly from:**

**Book Publishing Company • P.O. Box 99 • Summertown, TN 38483 • 1-800-695-2241**

*Please include $3.95 per book for shipping and handling.*